The
Disciplines
of Life

by

V. Raymond Edman, Ph.D., LL.D.
Former President, Wheaton College
Wheaton, Illinois

HARVEST HOUSE PUBLISHERS
1075 Arrowsmith, Eugene, Oregon 97402

Scripture quotations, unless otherwise noted, are taken from the King James Version.

Twelfth Printing.

THE DISCIPLINES OF LIFE

© 1982 Mrs. V. R. Edman
Reprinted by Harvest House Publishers
Eugene, Oregon 97402

ISBN 0-89081-276-4
Library of Congress Catalog Card Number 81-84813

Printed in the United States of America.

DEDICATION

Life's early lessons make indelible impressions on the plastic spirit of childhood. The great disciplines of life: to love God with all my heart, to receive the Lord Jesus Christ as my personal Saviour, to learn the sacred Scriptures, to serve God and my fellow men—these have come from my dear old mother, to whom I gratefully dedicate this little volume.

Acknowledgment is made for the gracious use in this book of poetry by the following copyright holders: Abingdon-Cokesbury Press; American Tract Society; Evangelical Publishers; Nimmo, Hay & Mitchell; Society for Promotion of Christian Knowledge.

For the use of other poems and quoted matter acknowledgment will be made on subsequent editions as ownership is identified.

V. R. EDMAN

"Westgate"
Wheaton College

PREFACE

Ours is an undisciplined age. The old disciplines are breaking down, and the foundations of society appear to be crumbling. The discipline of the home seems to be vanishing in the new psychology which teaches: parents obey your children! The discipline of the schoolroom is becoming anathema, according to the so-called Progressive Education, lest the personality of the child be thwarted by the imposition of a will higher than his own. The old academic "disciplines": mathematics, ancient language, grammar, are being ignored as obsolete and unimportant. Above all, the discipline of divine grace is derided as legalism or is entirely unknown to a generation that is largely illiterate in the Scriptures. We need the rugged strength of Christian character that can come only from discipline: the discipline of spirit, of mind, of body, of society. Otherwise, the home will lose its heart as well as its hearth, the schoolroom its strength, the textbooks their exactness, the Scriptures their sanction. Here are some disciplines of life presented to Wheaton's "brave sons and daughters true," that they be sturdy citizens of the Red, White and Blue, and especially, good soldiers of the Crimson Cross. I trust that the Disciplines will be helpful to you.

CONTENTS

Yes, to keep from growing weary and faint-hearted, just think of the example set by Him who has endured so great opposition aimed at Him by sinful men! You have not yet, as you have struggled on against sin, resisted to the point of pouring out your blood, and you have forgotten the encouragement which is addressed to you as sons:

"My son, refrain from thinking lightly of the discipline
　　the Lord inflicts,
　And giving up when you are corrected by Him.
　For He disciplines everyone He loves,
　And chastises every son whom He heartily receives."

Hebrews 12:5, 6 (Williams' translation)

You must submit to discipline. God is dealing with you as His sons. For who is the son that his father never disciplines?

FOREWORD

These very practical and thought-provoking chapters have been circulated through various channels for some months past and have brought blessing to many. It is a pleasure to commend them now that they are collected into one volume and sent forth to instruct and edify those who will take the time to read and meditate upon them. The general theme is one of great importance, often overlooked in this day of "self-expression" and vaunted intellectual freedom which often results, not in liberty alone but in license to indulge every selfish propensity. The beloved and honored president of Wheaton College has pointed the danger of unbridled behavior and of careless thinking and has pointed out the path of subjection to strong discipline which alone can produce lasting peace and true happiness. Do not dismiss this volume with a casual scanning of its pages but, "read, mark, and inwardly digest" its thoughtful contents, and life will be enriched thereby.

THE DISCIPLINE OF
DISCIPLESHIP

"If any man will come after me" (*Luke* 9:23).

Discipleship means "discipline!" The disciple is that one who has been taught or trained by the Master, who has come with his ignorance, superstition, and sin, to find learning, truth, and forgiveness from the Saviour. Without discipline we are not disciples, even though we profess His Name and pass for a follower of the lowly Nazarene. In an undisciplined age when liberty and license have replaced law and loyalty, there is greater need than ever before that we be disciplined to be His disciples.

Discipleship requires the discipline of *conversion*, wherein we recognize our lost estate because of rebellion against God, and with penitence come to the Saviour, the Lord Jesus Christ. We assent from our hearts that "all we like sheep have gone astray; we have turned every one to his own way" (Isa. 53:6), that "all have sinned, and come short of the glory of God" (Rom. 3:23), that "the Scripture hath concluded all under sin" (Gal. 3:22), and that we "were by nature the children of wrath, even as others . . . .

9

strangers from the covenants of promise, having no hope, and without God in the world" (Eph. 2:3,12).

This discipline is difficult for the natural heart of each one, for we will not humble ourselves to admit our sin and shame; but it is easy for the honest and good heart that sees itself in the light of Calvary's Sacrifice for sin. In the dispensation before the Cross, David, seeing himself, cried, "I have sinned against the Lord"; to which God replied through His servant, "the Lord also hath put away thy sin" (II Sam. 12:13). When Peter saw himself in the light of the Lord's presence and power, he fell down saying, "Depart from me; for I am a sinful man, O Lord" (Luke 5:8). A woman wept as she stood by His feet, which she washed with her tears of repentance; and she heard the Saviour's word, "Thy sins are forgiven . . . . thy faith hath saved thee; go in peace" (Luke 7:48,50). The penitent Publican smote his breast in genuine sorrow for sin, and prayed, "God be merciful to me a sinner" (Luke 18:13), and went home justified.

Thus it has been down the ages; the despondent, despairing of themselves, have come to the Saviour for mercy, and have been saved. "Not by works of righteousness which we have done, but according to his mercy he saved us" (Titus 3:5). "But as many as received him, to them gave he power to become the sons of God, even to them that believe on his name" (John 1:12). Without salvation no sonship; without sonship, no discipleship!

It is His sons whom God disciplines that they might bring honor to His name. He wants to teach and train them, to soften and sweeten them, to strengthen and steady them, that they may show forth the excellencies of Him who told them, "Learn of me; for I am meek and lowly in heart: and ye shall find rest unto your souls" (Matt. 11:29). Without discipline we are not His sons; but as His own we need the exhortation, "My son, despise not thou the chastening of the Lord, nor faint when thou art rebuked of him; for whom the Lord loveth he chasteneth, and scourgeth every son whom he receiveth" (Heb. 12:5,6). This discipline at the moment may not seem "to be joyous, but (rather) grievous: nevertheless afterward it yieldeth the peaceable fruit of righteousness unto them which are exercised thereby" (12:11).

Discipleship requires the discipline of *cost*. Our Lord's words search deeply into the depth of our souls, as He says, "He that loveth father or mother more than me is not worthy of me: and he that loveth son or daughter more than me is not worthy of me" (Matt. 10:37). On a later occasion He amplified that statement to divine principle by saying, "If any man come to me, and hate not his father, and mother, and wife, and children, and brethren, and sisters, yea, and his own life also, he cannot be my disciple" (Luke 14:26).

What can be the meaning of this strong, unsubdued standard, to "hate" all, even one's own life? We are to love and cherish parents, brothers, children; we love

11

others more because we belong to Christ. What then, does our Lord mean? Is it not, that we all, like Saul of Tarsus, truly "count all things but loss for the excellency of the knowledge of Christ Jesus my Lord: for whom I have suffered the loss of all things, and do count them but dung, that I may win Christ" (Phil. 3:8)? We are to make our Lord Jesus supreme, permanent, pre-eminent in our hearts, so that no person nor anything shares that place in our lives. No price of parents or loved ones, possessions or life itself, is too great for His sake.

This denial of all, including ourselves, is the deepest discipline of discipleship. There are those who are dearer to us than life itself; but they should not be dearer than the Saviour. For Him and His cause we have died to them and every other earthly creature or pleasure — it is Jesus only! Our Lord does not desire that we take this discipline lightly or thoughtlessly. He gives two strong illustrations about counting the cost (Luke 14:28-33), concluding, "So likewise, whosoever he be of you that forsaketh not all that he hath, he cannot be my disciple."

One remembers an earnest and effective layman in Ecuador who felt called to God's service in the ministry; but his wife would not hear of it. She threatened all manner of reprisal if he should leave his lucrative employment to become a servant of the Lord Jesus. One evening he came to me, with a bundle under one arm, and tears in his eyes. I turned to Mark 10, and read to him verses 29 and 30: "Verily I say unto you, There is no man that hath left house, or brethren, or sisters, or father, or mother, or wife, or children, or lands, for my sake, and the gospel's, but he shall receive an hundredfold now in this time, houses, and brethren, and sisters, and mothers, and children, and lands, with persecutions; and in the world to come eternal life."

After prayer and tears, I inquired, "And what have you in the bundle?"

"It contains my working clothes. I left my employment today." He had counted the cost, and had set himself to leave all, and to face whatever persecutions might come; only that he might be Jesus' disciple. And do we wonder that he won his wife to full allegiance to the Master, and that together they have become pillars in the house of God?

Discipleship requires the discipline of *cross-bearing*. Three things seem to be necessary for us each day: our daily food (for which we are to pray, Matt. 6:11); our daily work (in which we are to be faithful, I Thess. 4:11, 12; II Thess. 3:10-13), and our daily cross. Our Lord said, "If any man will come after me, let him deny himself, and take up his cross daily, and follow me" (Luke 9:23), "And whosoever doth not bear his cross, and come after me, cannot be my disciple" (Luke 14:27; Matt. 16:24).

This cross is not that of our Saviour, who suffered

once for our sins upon the Tree, for we add no part
to the price of our redemption; and least of all, is it
bearing an outward cross, around one's neck as we see
in America, or on one's shoulder, as I have seen in
Ethiopia. It is the denial of self, in the deepest meaning of that word, and of all that life has to offer, in
full surrender to the will of God; in the spirit of Calvary's Cross, to be sure. I find its depths to be
plumbed in the experience and language of others:

"I take, O Cross, thy shadow for my abiding
　　place;
I ask no other sunshine, than the sunshine of
　　His face;
Content to let the world go by, to know no
　　gain nor loss,
My sinful self my only shame, my glory, all
　　the Cross."[1]

"Whatever else Thou sendest, oh, send this —
Not ecstacy of love or lover's kiss,
But strength to know the joy of sacrifice,
To see life deeply as with opened eyes!
Oh, grant me this, dear God,
　　Through tears or loss —
To know the joyous secret
　　Of Thy Cross."[2]

---

[1] "Beneath the Cross of Jesus," by Elizabeth C. Clephane.
[2] "At Calvary," by Ralph Spaulding Cushman. *Hilltop Verses and Prayers,*
(Nashville: Abingdon-Cokesbury Press, 1945), p. 99.

Because of His Cross, not in addition to it, we are daily crucified unto the world and all that is therein of good or evil. To bear our cross, because of His, is to learn of Him, the Meek and Lowly in heart, and to be disciples.

One kneels humbly, perhaps bewildered and blinded with tears, beside the Teacher, who in tenderness and true love for our souls desires to teach us this discipline. The world dazzles us, but is dim in comparison with Him; loved ones allure, but He is the altogether Lovely One. His love has broken every barrier down, and we whisper, "Lord Jesus, at any Cost, by any Cross, make me Thy disciple."

15

Pressed

Pressed out of measure and pressed to all length,
Pressed so intently, it seems beyond strength,
Pressed in the body, and pressed in the soul,
Pressed in the mind till the dark surges roll,
Pressure by foes, and a pressure by friends,
Pressure on pressure till life nearly ends.

Pressed into knowing no helper but God,
Pressed into loving the staff and the rod,
Pressed into liberty where nothing clings,
Pressed into faith for impossible things,
Pressed into living a life in the Lord,
Pressed into living a Christ-life outpoured.
                    — Selected

THE DISCIPLINE OF
DANGER

"Should such a man as I flee?" (*Neh.* 6:11).

Life is continually beset by many dangers: physical dangers at home as well as on the highway or in the hospital; social dangers from within as well as from without; spiritual dangers from companions and customs as well as from carelessness or compromise. We cannot avoid dangers, even in the most sheltered circumstances; and our problem is detecting the dangers and facing them, avoiding them if possible, but never ignoring them.

Illustrative of the discipline of danger is the experience of Nehemiah, the cupbearer of the mightiest monarch of his day, who preferred to identify himself with the remnant of his people in the Land of Promise than to enjoy the leisure and luxury of the world. At great personal sacrifice he left the court, to be content with the hard lot of a pioneer in a country of desolation.

One would think that his sacrifice in leaving position and pleasure would have been sufficient for him, and for any servant of God, but that was not the case.

There were persistent and pestiferous foes in the land, who could not bear to see God's cause prosper; and they hated especially Nehemiah, who had come to assume leadership for the discouraged builders of Jerusalem. Any servant of God in a place of responsibility, however obscure or prominent that place might be, will have similar dogged and deceitful dangers. The Sanballats, Tobiahs and the Arabian Geshems did not cease to exist when the walls of Jerusalem were completed; rather, down the ages the leaders of the Lord's people have faced their cruel and cunning connivances.

There was the danger of *intrigue* (Neh. 6:1-4). In their machinations to do mischief unto Nehemiah they proposed a meeting in some village outside the city walls. Their plausible purpose was to come to an understanding, the one with the other, that all future difficulties could be avoided; their real objective was to put Nehemiah into a position of compromise, whereby he would be suspected by his compatriots, or to capture him by guile.

Our critics and enemies always have ostensible reasons for wanting to talk things over a bit. They are adept at raising questions and instilling doubts. They want us to explain our convictions and our course of action not for their enlightenment and edification, but for our confusion. It seems that we should make an answer, that we should defend ourselves by explaining our motives and our methods, that we should set right the thinking of our opponents in one strong statement of fact, that we should dispel all doubts by a definition of our divinely appointed duty. But such is never the case. If they really wanted information, enlightenment, statement of fact, they could come to us; but they desire only doubt, difficulty, diversion from duty, and disgrace to us.

Our strongest answer to intrigue is found in the course of action followed by Nehemiah. He weighed the alternatives in an even scale, and determined that he had been called to build, not to argue or to explain. He said simply and tersely, "I am doing a great work, so that I cannot come down: why should the work cease, whilst I leave it, to come down to you?" (Neh. 6:3). How great danger of intrigue would be avoided in God's service, and how much would be built, if we determined that it was also our duty not to neglect the work by descending to the plane of pestilential critics. To the work, and not to words!

There was also the subtle danger of *innuendo*. When the snare of deserting duty proved successful against the active and aggressive Nehemiah, his foes sought to discount his efforts by ascribing false motives to him (Neh. 6:5-9). There was the familiar technique of an "open letter" (vs. 5), in which "it is reported . . . that thou and the Jews think to rebel: for which cause thou buildest the wall, that thou mayest be their king" (vs. 6). Flight of imagination, false indications, fanciful implications—all are employed to make Nehemiah's motives subtle, selfish, and sordid. Unvarnished untruth, rumor run riot, downright deceit, nothing seems to be withheld from God's servant, to prevent his performing his appointed task.

Is there not an old, yet up-to-date ring about this accusation. Toward the dawn of human history did not the Enemy, the Father of lies (John 8:44) ascribe selfish objectives to Job, saying, "Doth Job fear God for nought?" (Job 1:9). Joseph's brethren said, "Behold, this dreamer cometh. Come now therefore, and let us slay him" (Gen. 37:19, 20). To Jeremiah, ardent patriot of Jerusalem and earnest prophet of Jehovah it was stoutly declared, "thou fallest away to the Chaldeans" (Jer. 37:13), and no denial of God's servant was able to reverse that false declaration. The Lord Jesus knew the biting bitterness of false accusation, by erudite Pharisees and their uninformed following, "He casteth out devils through Beelzebub the chief of devils" (Luke 11:15); "We found this fellow perverting the nation, and forbidding to give tribute to Caesar, saying that he himself is Christ a King . . . He stirreth up all the people" (23:2, 5). And who today has not had his motives misinterpreted, his methods maligned, his efforts endangered by insidious innuendo?

Nehemiah gives us the solution of this discipline. He says frankly, "There are no such things done as thou sayest, but thou feignest them out of thine own heart" (Neh. 6:8); and thereafter he commits his cause to Him who judgeth righteously. We are to trust, and not be afraid (Isa. 12:2). We can say with David, "For I have heard the slander of many: fear was on every side: while they took counsel together against me, they devised to take away my life. But I trusted in thee, O Lord: I said, Thou art my God. My times are in thy hand: deliver me from the hand of mine enemies, and from them that persecute me . . . Let the lying lips be put to silence; which speak grievous things proudly and contemptuously against the righteous" (Ps. 31:13-15, 18).

Intimidation follows unsuccessful intrigue and innuendo (Neh. 6:10-14). The Enemy is persistent in his plot to undo the work of the godly. Nehemiah was warned by the Mafia of his day, "Let us meet together in the house of God [how pious the fierce Prince of Darkness can become!], within the temple, and let us shut the doors of the temple: for they will come to slay thee; yea, in the night will they come to slay thee" (6:10).

Down the ages men and women have stood in the place of danger for God; and their stand has been honored by Him. Gideon, with three hundred, faced the hosts of Midian and Amalek, that "lay along in the valley like grasshoppers for multitude" (Judges 7:12), Shammah stood his ground when all fled, "and the Lord wrought a great victory" (II Sam. 23:12). Asa, before the onslaught of a vast horde of Ethiopians, prayed, "Lord, it is nothing with thee to help, whether with many, or with them that have no power: help us, O Lord our God; for we rest on thee, and in thy name we go against this multitude" (II Chron. 14:11). Jehoshaphat cried, "O our God, wilt thou not judge them? for we have no might against this great company that cometh against us; neither know we what to do: but our eyes are upon thee" (II Chron. 20:12). Three young men declared, "If it be so, our God whom we serve is able to deliver us from the burning fiery furnace, and he will deliver us out of thine hand, O king. But if not, be it known unto thee, O king, that we will not serve thy gods, nor worship the golden image which thou hast set up" (Dan. 3: 17, 18).

Nehemiah's reply to intimidation is worthy of record, "Should such a man as I flee? . . . I will not go in" (Neh. 6:11). Are we servants of the Most High, and should we fear to stand firm in His cause, in nothing terrified by our adversaries? (Phil. 1:28).

Intrigue, innuendo and intimidation are insufficient to terrify and drive backward the soldier of the Cross, clad in the armor of righteousness (Eph. 6:10-18); so *insinuation* is substituted by the insistent and insatiable Adversary of our soul. "Moreover in those days the nobles of Judah sent many letters unto Tobiah, and the letters of Tobiah came unto them . . . Also they reported his good deeds before me, and uttered my words to him. And Tobiah sent letters to put me in fear" (Neh. 6:17, 19). Letters, letters, letters, how they are multiplied against the servant of God, as in Nehemiah's day, even by "the nobles." Few seem too high-principled not to stoop to writing letters about others, "many letters," with their sinuous and sly insinuations. What havoc they wreak in God's cause, what heartache they produce. One of the deepest testings of a true child of God is to stick to his divinely appointed duty when all the while there is a barrage of letters about him.

Intrigue, innuendo, intimidation, insinuation, those constitute the discipline of danger. Our temptation is to turn from our task to untangle the intrigue, to take time to undo the innuendo, to flee from intimidation and to fight hidden insinuation. Our safety is in doing our duty, (2:3), in putting our trust in God (6:9), in standing stedfast and immovable (6:11), and in serving in silence. The result for us will be as it was with Nehemiah, "the wall was finished . . . our enemies . . . were much cast down in their own eyes: for they perceived that this work was wrought of our God" (6:15, 16). Danger feared is folly, danger faced is freedom.

Stand — withstand

Stand still! Stand firm!
  Stand ever sound—
Stand armour clad,
  'Tis fighting ground;
Then stand with victor's grip,
  The "foe" to overthrow;
With holy hands, unloose the bands—
  'Tis Christ that brought him low.
—Evan Roberts

THE DISCIPLINE OF
DARING

"Only be thou strong and very courageous" (*Josh.* 1:7).

THEODORE ROOSEVELT'S favorite chapter in the Bible was the first chapter of Joshua; and not without cause. The Rough Rider was always a man of action, in the ranch lands of the Dakotas, in the politics of the Empire State, on the slopes of San Juan Hill, in the diplomacy of the White House that talked gently but carried a big stick. He knew that life required character and courage.

To be sure, there is the discipline of deliberation, wherein one ponders the pathway he should take and restudies the resources he will need for any given enterprise; but there is also the discipline of daring, wherein one decides to do his duty despite every difficulty and danger. To deliberate unduly can mean to delay until doubt paralyzes one's powers; to dare, when God is for us and is leading us, is to defy the human impossibilities until the outcome is complete triumph. Daring can mean the difference between defeat by default and the delight of duty well done.

Like Joshua, we have need of the exhortation, "Only be thou strong and very courageous" (1:7). There are *giants* now as then, that join forces against us because we are the people of God. They had been seen by Joshua when with others he had spied out the Promised Land (Num. 13). Joshua did not deny their presence in the land, nor depreciate their power; but he could not concur in the opinion of the majority that, "There we saw the giants, . . . and we were in our own sight as grasshoppers, and so were we in their sight" (Num. 13:33). The children of God as grasshoppers because of some giants? "Ridiculous!" thought Joshua, and Caleb with him. "If the Lord delight in us, then he will bring us into this land, and give it us; a land which floweth with milk and honey. Only rebel not ye against the Lord, neither fear ye the people of the land; for they are bread for us: their defence is departed from them, and the Lord is with us: fear them not!" (14:8,9).

Daring sees God, not the giants; the Saviour, not the "cities walled up to heaven"; the promises, not the impossibilities; the authority of God, not the Anakim. Daring says with Caleb and Joshua, "Let us go up at once, and possess it; for we are well able to overcome it" (13:30). Daring finds that there is more danger of defeat from the faint-hearted and fearful in one's own ranks than from fierce foes who may be as huge as giants. The despairing were in the majority, for ten spies reported, "We be not able to go up against

26

the people; for they are stronger than we" (13:31); the daring were only two, who could affirm stoutly, "We are well able" (v. 30). Daring often stands alone or in a hopeless minority; and learns therein one of the primary lessons of patience that leads to triumph: dread not the majority that outvotes you nor the mob that would stone you (14:10). Happy is the heart that has learned the strong confidence of Hebrews 13:5,6: ". . . for he hath said, I will never leave thee, nor forsake thee. So that we may boldly say, The Lord is my helper, and I will not fear what man shall do unto me." Dare to count upon God's presence with you!

Daring may be delayed by the counsel of the cautious, but its moment of opportunity comes at long length. Like Joshua, we stand at the border of a promised land, wherein still dwell giants, and we are told, "Only be thou strong and very courageous." As we venture forth at God's Word, we find that our real foes are not the fierce sons of Anak, but rather are the furtive Achans within our own camp (Josh. 7). The self-seeking, self-pleasing, self-centered selfishness within us that disregards the commandment of God to separation from worldly acclaim or achievement of any kind; these are the real giants to be conquered. If they are not first overcome within us by the power of God, then we are powerless before small cities like Ai, not to speak of larger and more lordly ones. Devotion to duty, obedience to God's Word, separation from known sin, these must precede daring; and without them, the stoutest heart is powerless. The genuine giants are within us, the awe-inspiring Anakim are among us; and not until they have been put to the Sword of the Spirit can we assay to go forth against the citadels of sin and Satan. There is a discipline of daring: to be strong and very courageous, whatever giant may join battle against us.

There is the *Jordan,* as well as the giants, to hinder us, as it did Joshua. The giants may represent spiritual and psychological foes that face us when we would follow God; the Jordan may well represent physical factors that render fortuitous or even foolish any thought of following Him further. To be sure, God has brought us from the iron furnace of Egypt, through certain death at the Red Sea; and has led by fiery pillar and fed by unfailing manna. With the children of Israel we have come to know the reality of Psalm 78:72: "So he fed them according to the integrity of his heart; and guided them by the skilfulness of his hands." But the Jordan is a different difficulty from that of the wilderness, we declare. It is untrodden and treacherous, and "overfloweth all his banks all the time of harvest" (Josh. 3:15). It is without any bridge or ford, without any promise of passageway; rather, it is only a raging torrent that terrifies and intimidates.

There are physical factors that make impossible our obedience to the known will of God. The Lord's word was, "Arise, go over this Jordan, thou, and all this people" (1:2); but the Jordan was unchanged by that command. Caution counsels, "Consider the matter carefully, from every angle. Do not presume upon the power and providence of God. He is leading you, He will bring you to a bridge." It is true that we are not to be presumptuous; for even the Lord Jesus, under pressure to presume upon the promise of God, repeated the Word, "Thou shalt not tempt the Lord thy God" (Matt. 4:7, Deut. 6:16). God had not commanded our Lord to leap from the pinnacle of the temple in order to test the provision of angelic help; and furthermore, there was a staircase leading down to the pavement. On the contrary, however, God had told Joshua to "go over this Jordan," just as it was. There is a very fine line of differentiation between fanaticism of self-will and the faith of obedience to God's will; and happy the heart that learns that difference.

While caution considers and deliberation delays, daring obeys the explicit command of the Lord. The fearful and faint-hearted do not know the quickening of pulse and the confidence in a Presence that comes with the obedience venturing to put one's feet into overflowing impossibility; and to find a way where there seems to be none.

"And as they that bore the ark were come unto Jordan, and the feet of the priests that bore the ark dipped in the brim of the water, . . . the waters which came down from above stood and rose up upon an heap . . . and all the Israelites passed over on dry ground"

(3:15-17). This is a discipline of daring: to be strong when the seeming impossibility stares one in the face; to be very courageous when obedience commands that we put our feet on the brim of certain disaster. That discipline has many memorials to God's mercy, as had Joshua in the heaps of stones within the Jordan and along its side, to testify, "It was here that God helped me." Daring is doing the will of God!

Jericho, as well as the giants and the Jordan, may jeer at us when we obey God. Why must there be one impossibility after another in the pathway of faith and obedience: the fear of giants, then the fury of the Jordan, and now the fortress of Jericho? It is because it is a life of faith, and not one of sight. It is faith that follows God implicitly, albeit with trembling on occasion; and not the sight that calculates, considers, cautions, and cringes. Daring is always on a miracle basis; deliberation is on the allegedly safe ground of human ability. Paul knew the pressure upon pressure of the impossible, even unto human despair, "that we should not trust in ourselves, but in God which raiseth the dead: Who delivered us from so great a death, and doth deliver: in whom we trust that he will yet deliver us" (II Cor. 1:9, 10). He could testify, "We are troubled on every side, yet not distressed; we are perplexed, but not in despair; Persecuted, but not forsaken; cast down, but not destroyed" (II Cor. 4:8, 9). Why? Because he knew the overcoming and sustaining power of the indwelling Christ (vs. 10). To walk by faith is to face an unending succession of giants, Jordans, and Jerichos; and to dare is to conquer each one in turn.

Whatever may be our Jericho, it will not jeer at us indefinitely, if we obey the word and will of our God. Its walls may be high, its battlements formidable, its strength undoubted, its occupants unyielding; but prayer and patience will bring it low before the soul that dares to obey God. God's methods may not be ours—usually are not. At Jericho it was the silent march of the host for days, and then the shout of faith that brought the victory (Josh. 6:16, 20). At Ai, it was Joshua's spear stretched forth that symbolized the faith that obeys and triumphs (8:18, 26). Centuries later the children of Israel sang at the commandment of King Jehoshaphat; and their song secured the conquest of their foes (II Chron. 20:22). Silence or shout, spear or song, or any other divinely-appointed manner of service is effective in the hand of those who dare to trust and to obey.

This is the discipline of daring: to discern one's duty, to do God's bidding, to delight in His presence, to depend upon His promise, to discover His power as we obey His word, "Only be thou strong and very courageous, that thou mayest observe to do . . . that thou mayest prosper whithersoever thou goest. . . . Have not I commanded thee? Be strong and of a good courage; be not afraid, neither be thou dismayed: for the Lord thy God is with thee whithersoever thou goest" (Josh. 1:7, 9).

O for a faith that will not shrink,
    Tho' pressed by every foe,
That will not tremble on the brink
    Of any earthly woe!

That will not murmur nor complain
    Beneath the chastening rod,
But, in the hour of grief or pain,
    Will lean upon its God;

A faith that shines more bright and clear
    When tempests rage without
That when in danger knows no fear,
    In darkness feels no doubt.

              — William H. Bathurst.

THE DISCIPLINE OF
DARKNESS

"That walketh in darkness, and hath no light?"
(Isa. 50:10).

THERE IS profound and practical truth in the statement, "Never doubt in the dark what God told you in the light." This statement implies that it is possible for the child of God to "be filled with the knowledge of his will in all wisdom and spiritual understanding" (Col. 1:9), and "understanding what the will of the Lord is" (Eph. 5:17). We are admonished in Romans 12:1,2, to be living sacrifices, not conformed to this world, "transformed by the renewing of your mind, that ye may prove what is that good, and acceptable, and perfect, will of God." It is entirely possible for the child of God in the light of the Word, by the gracious guidance of the Holy Spirit, by obedience to the light given by God, to be persuaded of the will of God, much as the Apostle Paul was told, "Be of good cheer, Paul: for as thou hast testified of me in Jerusalem, so must thou bear witness also at Rome" (Acts 23:11). After such revelation of the will of God, there seems to come with eternal inevitability "the trial of your faith, being much more

precious than of gold that perisheth" (I Pet. 1:7).
Paul was a prisoner, suffered shipwreck, and was given
up for dead before he reached Rome, but he arrived,
according to the promise of God. This trial of faith
provides the discipline of darkness for God's child,
that he may learn to trust his Father in the shadow
as well as in the sunshine.

Joseph learned that discipline in his life. In the
quiet and shelter of his childhood home he had come
to know by dreams and visions that he was to have
a place of pre-eminence among his older brothers. His
pathway led through hatred, envy, and rejection by
his own, who sold him into slavery in Egypt. Menial
service and murderous misrepresentation were his lot
in Potiphar's house, and in the prison he was forgotten
of men, but not of God. He endured the discipline
of darkness because, "Until the time that his word
came to pass, the word of the Lord tried him" (Ps.
105:19, R.V.). That discipline sweetened him so that,
at the summit of his success, when all Egypt was
subject to his word, he could say to his brethren,
"But as for you, ye thought evil against me: but God
meant it unto good, to bring to pass, as it is this day,
to save much people alive" (Gen. 50:20). The dreams
of youth, disciplined by darkness, made it possible
for him to perform magnanimously the prerogatives
of power.

Jeremiah came to know this discipline. When mis-
understood and misrepresented by others, he received

the assurance of his Lord, "Verily it shall be well with thy remnant; verily I will cause the enemy to entreat thee well in the time of evil and in the time of affliction. . . . They shall fight against thee, but they shall not prevail against thee: for I am with thee to save thee and to deliver thee, saith the Lord" (Jer. 15:11,20). After he had received that gracious promise, he went deeper into distress and difficulty, into the dungeon, and into danger of death both from the citizens of the city and from the enemy outside the walls. When the city was taken, however, Jeremiah heard anew, "But I will deliver thee in that day, saith the Lord: and thou shalt not be given into the hand of the men of whom thou art afraid. For I will surely deliver thee, and thou shalt not fall by the sword, but thy life shall be for a prey unto thee: because thou hast put thy trust in me, saith the Lord" (39:17,18). The dungeon was no place in which to doubt that deliverance was at hand.

John the Baptist knew this discipline in another way. John was "a burning and a shining light" (John 5:35), and great multitudes were attracted by his fiery preaching. In the days of his popularity and power he said of the Lord Jesus, "He must increase, but I must decrease" (John 3:30). Very possibly he did not know that "decrease" would lead to the hatred of implacable Herodias, to the dungeon, and finally to ignominious death. His perplexity in the darkness is expressed by his question sent by way of his disciples to the Lord, "Art thou he that should come, or do we look for another?" (Matt. 11:3). In response to such deep travail of soul, the Lord Jesus replied, "Blessed is he, whosoever shall not be offended in me" (vs.6). The discipline of darkness would cause us to be offended ("to stumble"); but there is a gracious possibility that we can be so established in the will of God that we will not doubt in the dark what was told us in the light.

Above many, Job came to know this discipline. He had walked in the light, upright before men and approved by God (Job 1:1,8), a man of deep personal piety (vs.5) and of great earthly prosperity (vs.3). Twice it was said of him by the Most High, "Hast thou considered my servant Job, that there is none like him in the earth, a perfect and an upright man, one that feareth God, and escheweth evil?" (1:8; 2:3). Suddenly he was plunged into dismay, desolation, disease, and despair.

There is the "dark night of the soul" for some of God's true children; a prolonged and painful period when God seems to be altogether absent, when health is gone, when friends forsake or aggravate, when days are dark and nights are long, when tomorrow holds no promise of light or alleviation from hopelessness, when the rest of the grave is preferred to the wearisome round of suffering and sorrow. Was human heart ever more disconsolate than that of Job, who complained constantly: "Why is light given to a man whose way is hid, and whom God hath hedged in?"

(3:23). "Oh, that I might have my request . . . . even that it would please God to destroy me" (6:8,9). "If I wash myself with snow water, and make my hands never so clean; Yet shalt thou plunge me in the ditch, and mine own clothes shall abhor me" (9: 30,31). "Wherefore hidest thou thy face, and holdest me for thine enemy? Wilt thou break a leaf driven to and fro? and wilt thou pursue the dry stubble?" (13:24,25).

The darkness brings to us haunting shadows that insinuate, "God has forgotten to be gracious," "God concerns not Himself with you," "God's will would not bring you into the shadow," "God has forsaken you because you have disobeyed Him," and a thousand similar subtle snares of Satan. On the contrary, the discipline of darkness can show us the wonderful truth of Isaiah 50:10, "Who is among you that feareth the Lord, that obeyeth the voice of His servant, that walketh in darkness, and hath no light? let him trust in the name of the Lord, and stay upon his God." Trust Him and Him alone; stay upon Him when all else fails. Our temptation is to give up all hope in the dark or else to kindle a fire of our own (Isa. 50:11) which will prove to be loss and sorrow. Rather, we find as heart and mind are stayed upon the Lord, that "Unto the upright there ariseth light in the darkness: he is gracious, and full of compassion, and righteous" (Ps. 112:4).

This is the discipline of darkness: *Never doubt in the dark what God told you in the light.*

O Jesus, I Have Promised

O Jesus, I have promised
To serve Thee to the end;
Be Thou forever near me,
My Master and my Friend:
I shall not fear the battle
If Thou art by my side,
Nor wander from the pathway
If Thou wilt be my guide.

Oh, let me feel Thee near me;
The world is ever near.
I see the sights that dazzle,
The tempting sounds I hear.
My foes are ever near me.
Around me and within;
But, Jesus, draw Thou nearer,
And shield my soul from sin.

O Jesus, Thou hast promised
To all who follow Thee,
That where Thou art in glory
There shall Thy servant be;
And, Jesus, I have promised
To serve Thee to the end.
Oh! give me grace to follow,
My Master and my Friend.

                    —John E. Bode.

THE DISCIPLINE OF
DECISION

"We will obey the voice of the Lord our God"
(*Jer.* 42:6).

Quite possibly you are standing at a fork in life's pathway and do not know whether you should turn to the right or to the left? Perhaps the decision that must be made today, or tomorrow at the latest, seems somewhat trivial; nevertheless, you sense intuitively that great issues are involved. You may never come again to this same parting of the ways, and life will be different in the tomorrows because of the decision of today. You feel the need of wisdom that is higher than your own; of guidance by the One who sees the end from the beginning, of grace that will be sufficient for you, and of faithfulness that will not fail. Life's great issues are settled by options that may seem to be unimportant, but which in reality constitute great crises.

The Scriptures give abundant promise of guidance to the trusting Christian. The Most High says to us, "I will instruct thee and teach thee in the way which thou shalt go: I will guide thee with mine eye." (Ps.

32:8). "The meek will he guide in judgment: and the meek will he teach his way" (Ps. 25:9). And there are numerous similar promises. In an incident related in Jeremiah 42, we trace God's provision of guidance, and we note there three outstanding factors that determine the discipline of decision.

1. *A willingness to ask guidance of God.* The remnant in Jerusalem came to Jeremiah with the request that "the Lord thy God may shew us the way wherein we may walk, and the thing that we may do" (vs.3). In this we must remember, "If any of you lack wisdom, let him ask of God, that giveth to all men liberally, and upbraideth not; and it shall be given him" (Jas. 1:5). Many have sought the Lord their God that He would lead them aright: Moses at the Red Sea, Joshua at the passage of the Jordan, Ruth in the village of Bethlehem, David in the wilderness, Nehemiah in the court of the king, Jeremiah in the prison, Peter on the housetop, and Paul on board the storm-tossed sailing craft. They all cried unto their Guide, who led them by the right way.

Willingness to ask implies a request made in all honesty on our part and in all faith in our faithful God. We must be willing to say, "Whether it be good, or whether it be evil, we will obey the voice of the Lord our God . . . . that it may be well with us, when we obey the voice of the Lord our God" (Jer. 42:6). With our short sight we cannot determine what in the long run will be for our benefit or for our detriment, and we must leave the choice with Him. We need the heart attitude of the Psalmist: "I will hear what God the Lord will speak: for he will speak peace unto his people, and to his saints: but let them not turn again to folly" (Ps. 85:8). On our part it must be an asking "in faith, nothing wavering. For he that wavereth is like a wave of the sea driven with the wind and tossed" (Jas. 1:6). Asking guidance of God implies committal, yielding, and assurance on our part that He will do as He has promised.

2. *A willingness to wait for God's guidance.* The answer to the impatient inhabitants of Judah did not come to Jeremiah the moment after they had asked him to pray to God for them; nor did it come the next day. Rather, "It came to pass after ten days, that the word of the Lord came unto Jeremiah" (42: 7). Have we patience to wait God's time and way of answering our prayer for guidance? Time has a way of sifting values, of changing circumstances, of altering objectives. On occasion we find ourselves in the valley of decision, where it seems imperative to us that the choice should be made at once; nevertheless we read, "Blessed are all they that wait for him" (Isa. 30:18). We are further assured that "they shall not be ashamed that wait for me" (Isa. 49:23). For the time being we may walk in darkness as did Job who said, "Behold, I go forward, but he is not there; and backward, but I cannot perceive him: on the left hand, where he doth work, but I cannot behold him: he hideth himself on the right hand, that I cannot see

him: But he knoweth the way that I take: when he hath tried me, I shall come forth as gold" (Job 23:8-10). There is strength and assurance for the trusting soul that will stand unafraid on the assertion, "He that believeth shall not make haste" (Isa. 28:16). God will not arrive too late, nor with too little for our deepest need.

3. *A willingness to obey the will of God,* as it is revealed to us. The word to the remnant in Jeremiah's day was, "If ye will still abide in this land, then will I build you, and not pull you down" (Jer. 42:10). To be sure, that was exactly the message they did not want to hear. Secretly they desired to flee into the land of Egypt where they would see neither pestilence nor warfare; yet they wanted God's approval of their preference.

Are you truly willing to obey the voice of the Lord, "whether it be good, or whether it be evil" to your way of thinking? To insist upon your preferment is to learn with sorrow in days to come that "the sword, which ye feared, shall overtake you there in the land of Egypt, and the famine, whereof ye were afraid, shall follow close after you there in Egypt; and there ye shall die" (42:16). On the other hand, to endure the chastening of the Lord, likened in this story to the captivity in Babylon, is to learn, "I will shew mercies unto you" (42:12). There is no substitute for wholehearted, implicit, immediate obedience to the revealed will of God. "To obey is better than sacrifice . . . For rebellion is as the sin of witchcraft, and stubbornness is as iniquity and idolatry" (I Sam. 15:22,23). "If ye be willing and obedient, ye shall eat the good of the land" (Isa. 1:19).

Again you remember that you stand at a fork in the road. You will find that to ask wisdom of the Highest, to wait for His indication of the way, and to obey Him without hesitation is to be led in the right way, at His time, and for His glory.

> With thoughtless and
> Impatient hands
> We tangle up
> The plans
> The Lord hath wrought.

> And when we cry
> In pain, He saith,
> "Be quiet, dear,
> While I untie the knot."

I Want The Faith

I want the faith
That envies not
The passing of the days;
That sees all times and ways
More endless than the stars;
That looks at life,
Not as a little day
Of heat and strife,
But one eternal revel of delight
With God, the Friend, Adventurer, and Light.

What matter if one chapter nears the end?
What matter if the silver deck the brow?
Chanting I go
Past crimson flaming
From the autum hills,
Past winter's snow,
To find that glad new chapter
Where God's spring
Shall lift its everlasting voice to sing.
This is the faith I seek;
It shall be mine,
A faith that looks beyond the peaks of time!

—Ralph Spaulding Cushman. *

*From SPIRITUAL HILLTOPS by Ralph S. Cushman. Copyright 1932
Used by permission of the publishers, Abingdon-Cokesbury Press.

THE DISCIPLINE OF
DECLINING DAYS

"And it came to pass, when Samuel was old . . ."
(*I Sam.* 8:1).

THERE ARE disciplines of childhood: diligence to obey parents and decision to accept the gospel invitation; of adolescence: dependability, delight, determination, and discipleship; of mature years: duty, darkness, delay, diversion, distinction; there is also that of old age. It is different from earlier disciplines; nevertheless, just as real, with results for good or ill that can help or hinder the rising generation. Samuel, the last of the judges of Israel, affords an excellent illustration of this discipline of declining days.

Declining years bring decrease of activities and responsibilities. The Tireless Thirties and Roaring Forties have given way to the Sensible Sixties and the Slackening Seventies. To grow old gracefully and graciously is a triumph; not to do so is a tragedy. There are those who will never admit to themselves or to others that they have passed the period of their effectiveness and service; and with hard hand and harsh voice they insist upon their place and position, which long since they have ceased to fill. They can be a grief to themselves and an aggravation unto others; while all the time by facing the facts squarely and sweetly they could be a benediction and blessing to all. One remembers the sage observations of Solomon, "The hoary head is a crown of glory, if it be found in the way of righteousness" and "The glory of young men is their strength: and the beauty of old men is the grey head" (Prov. 16:31, 20:29). One remembers also Browning's words,

> Grow old along with me!
> The best is yet to be
> The last of life, for which the first was made:
> Our times are in His hand
> Who saith "A whole I planned,
> Youth shows but half; trust God: see all nor be afraid!"
> But I need, now as then,
> Thee, God, who mouldest men;
> And since, not even while the whirl was worst,
> Did I, — to the wheel of life
> With shapes and colors rife,
> Bound dizzily, — mistake my end, to slake Thy thirst:
> So, take and use Thy work:
> Amend what flaws may lurk,
> What strain o' the stuff, what warpings past the aim!
> My times be in Thy hand!
> Perfect the cup as planned!
> Let age approve of youth, and death
> complete the same![1]

---

[1] "Rabbi Ben Ezra."

In that regard it is well that men and women in their mature years begin to plan for decreasing responsibilities when that day comes, so that they can adjust themselves without hurt of heart to themselves or harm to others. The best illustration of that foresight, and the lovely fruits thereof, I have seen on Wheaton campus. While still a young man, he observed that some old men cling to their position too long for their good or that of the work; with the result that he determined, should God spare his life, he would resign his college presidency at sixty, to devote himself loyally to teaching again; at seventy, he would decline all administrative heartaches and headaches, and devote his last active days to decreasing class schedule. One remembers his announcement, with a twinkle in his eye, "Now I am threescore and ten; and I want nothing more of department chairmanship or heavy committee responsibilities." Does anyone wonder that he was the "Grand Old Man" of the campus, mellow and mature in his understanding of history, kindly and constructive in his counsel and prayer with students, enthusiastic and active in his attendence at athletic contests, sensible and sagacious in his advice to faculty and administration? He had planned to grow old graciously, and accepted the discipline of declining duties as it came.

A major difficulty in the discipline of graciously granting responsibilities unto younger men and women is the feeling of not being wanted any longer. Samuel had served his people over the span of a long life. As a child he had been consecrated to the service of God and country; and "all Israel from Dan even to Beersheba knew that Samuel was established to be a prophet of the Lord" (I Sam. 3:20). For more than threescore years he bore willingly and patiently, the burden and grief of leadership for Israel (7:15-17); until as an old man he faced the demand of the elders of his people, "Behold, thou art old, and thy sons walk not in thy ways: now make us a king to judge us like all the nations" (8:5). He, who had served so long and so unselfishly (see 12:3-5), was no longer wanted in that position. Sad the old heart that sinks under ingratitude and indifference; and by the same token, happy the heart that has learned like Samuel to bring every matter to the Most High. "And Samuel prayed unto the Lord" (8:6). The Lord has a way of answering His trusted servant (8:7-9), and keeping him useful, as we shall see, under the shadow of His hand.

It was also a difficulty to Samuel that his sons walked not in his footsteps. As a little child, he had heard in the stillness of the night the statement of God against the carelessness of Eli, "because his sons made themselves vile, and he restrained them not" (3:13). He had seen defeat of Israel at Aphek (4:1-10), and the resultant death of Eli and his sons (4:11-18). For some reason or other, he too had been unsuccessful in training his sons to assume the tasks that some day he would have to lay down. Much cruelty can be committed in judging Samuel on insufficient evidence, or any father, for that matter, whose sons are not his equal. If sons and daughters sensed the sorrows and shame that their aged parents can feel when they follow not in the ways of God, they would bestir themselves spiritually and every other way, I am sure. "A wise son heareth his father's instruction: but a scorner heareth not rebuke. . . . A wise son maketh a glad father: but a foolish man despiseth his mother" (Prov. 13:1; 15:20). By way of contrast, who can measure the joy and pleasure of parents whose sons follow their father, as I have seen, in ministry or industry, profession or other calling. Solomon added, "The father of the righteous shall greatly rejoice: and he that begetteth a wise child shall have joy of him. Thy father and thy mother shall be glad, and she that bare thee shall rejoice" (Prov. 23:24,25).

A further difficulty for old Samuel was the adaptation to demands of a new day. He had succeeded Eli as judge in Israel; and they had followed a long succession of judges, whose office had been instituted of God after the death of Joshua (Judges 2:16). The nation long had been content with its political organization: a theocracy, with the judge as Jehovah's representative. Now they demanded a king, to be like the other nations of the earth (I Sam. 8:5). Instinctively Samuel felt that not only he was being set aside by his people, but God also was being rejected by them. That concern was corroborated by the word of the Lord, "for they have not rejected thee, but they have rejected me, that I should not reign over them" (8:7).

It seems to me that God had planned to provide a king for Israel, in His time and when His man was ready (see Deut. 17:14,15). It is my persuasion that David was that man, one after God's own heart (I Sam. 13:14; 16:7, 12). Samuel's life span reached until David's manhood (25:1); and if Israel had not been impatient, they need never have suffered under Saul. In vain did Samuel protest to the people that a king would be a luxury to them, a taskmaster and tax-gatherer (8:11-18). "The people refused to obey the voice of Samuel; and they said, Nay; but we will have a king over us; That we also may be like all the nations; . . . . And the Lord said to Samuel, Hearken unto their voice, and make them a king" (8:19,20,22).

It is a dark and difficult discipline of declining days to see the next generation turn from tried paths and tested principles to untrodden pathways. Like Samuel one can give his advice with earnest, even tearful admonition (8:11-18; 12:6-17). He can remind them of the efficacy of the old ways, of the hand of God in their national history, of the dangers of new political or religious theory and practice. Perhaps they will not listen, as was true of Israel. Rather than becoming sullen, scolding, sensitive or sentimental, one can have the sweetness and sincerity of Samuel, saying, "Yet turn not aside from following the Lord, but serve the Lord with all your heart; . . . . For the

Lord will not forsake his people for his great name's sake: because it hath pleased the Lord to make you his people. Moreover as for me, God forbid that I should sin against the Lord in ceasing to pray for you: but I will teach you the good and the right way" (12:20,22,23).

To pray and to teach! This word of Samuel brings us to the deepest discipline of declining days. When days of active service are done; when prominence becomes obscurity; favor, forgetfulness; association, solitude; service, silence; strength, senility; usefulness, apparent uselessness; then it is comforting to know and challenging to experience newer kinds of service. In my opinion, Samuel did more for Israel in the days of retirement than in all the long years of active and conspicuous service. He prayed for his people and their new king, in days that were darker and more difficult than any they had known under Samuel's administration. Who can measure the efficacy and effectiveness of his prayers? The Divine Record states succinctly, "Moses and Aaron among his priests, and Samuel among them that call upon his name; they called upon the Lord, and he answered them" (Ps. 99:6). Who would have thought that the divine epitaph of Samuel would include him as an intercessor like the lawgiver?

God's patriarchs, no longer preoccupied with the problems of the present, can pray for this new generation, that it walk in God's way. Abraham prayed for

Isaac, Ishmael, and Lot; Jacob for his sons and their households (Gen. 48; 49); Moses for Israel that they be not shepherdless (Num. 27:15-17); Samuel for Israel and Saul; Elisha for Samaria (II Kings 13:14-20). Listen to an old man, spent with many years of service for God and man, in the darkness and dampness of a prison cell as he prays, "For this cause I bow my knees unto the Father of our Lord Jesus Christ, of whom the whole family in heaven and earth is named, That he would grant you, according to the riches of his glory, to be strengthened with might by his Spirit in the inner man; That Christ may dwell in your hearts by faith . . . " (Eph. 3:14-17). He could say, "I thank my God upon every remembrance of you, Always in every prayer of mine for you all making request with joy, For your fellowship in the gospel from the first day until now; Being confident of this very thing, that he which hath begun a good work in you will perform it until the day of Jesus Christ . . . " (Phil. 1:3-6). The prison prayers of Paul for the Christians of that day, who can measure their power! Or who can measure the might of the prayers of men and women no longer active in service for God and man who say, "God forbid that I should sin against the Lord in ceasing to pray for you"!

Or in teaching! It seems reasonable to understand from the Scriptural account that Samuel had been so busy with administration that he had been unable to give much time and effort to teaching. The two func-

tions are quite different. Now that he was no longer
to be the leader of his people, he could pray and he
could teach. It appears in the history of Israel that
Samuel gathered around him young men who were
taught in the Scriptures, and who became "prophets"
among their people (I Sam. 19:18-20). Thus began the
"school of the prophets" (II Kings 2:15; 4:38; 6:1);
which institution had a lasting influence for spiritual-
ity and godliness, in the centuries after Samuel. Thus
it appears that Samuel accomplished increased lasting good for his people in the days of obscurity following his retirement from public office, for then
came the opportunity to teach and to pray as never
before.

The discipline of declining days that comes when
days wane and strength subsides, when doors close
and comforters depart, when others bear the heat
and the burden of the day; then to grow old graciously
and sweetly; to grant responsibilities to stronger,
though less experienced hands of our sons or those
of others; to adapt oneself to the demands of a new
day; and above all, to pray for others and to serve
the Lord in whatever hidden ministry may be ours.
Thus disciplined in spirit we are sweetness and
strength to those who need us most.

When God wants to drill a man,
And thrill a man,
And skill a man,
When God wants to mold a man
To play the noblest part;
When He yearns with all His heart
To create so great and bold a man
That all the world shall be amazed,
Watch His methods, watch His ways!
How He ruthlessly perfects
Whom He royally elects!
How He hammers him and hurts him,
And with mighty blows converts him
Into trial shapes of clay which
Only God understands;
While his tortured heart is crying
And he lifts beseeching hands!
How He bends but never breaks
When his good He undertakes;
How He uses whom He chooses,
And with every purpose fuses him;
By every act induces him
To try His splendor out —
God knows what He's about.

THE DISCIPLINE OF

DEFAMATION

"Let him alone, and let him curse . . . it may be that the Lord will . . . requite me good for his cursing this day" (II Sam. 16:11, 12).

Iᴛ ɪꜱ ᴜɴᴅᴇʀꜱᴛᴀɴᴅᴀʙʟᴇ that we should take patiently and graciously whatever correction we need, and to take rebuke for our errors; "but if, when ye do well, and suffer for it, ye take it patiently, this is acceptable with God" (I Pet. 2:20). When we want to answer back, to return the abuse that we have received with interest added, to defend ourselves and our actions, where motives and methods were above reproach, then we are to remember, "for this is thankworthy, if a man for conscience toward God endure grief, suffering wrongfully . . . For even hereunto were ye called: because Christ also suffered for us, leaving us an example, that ye should follow his steps . . . Who, when he was reviled, reviled not again; when he suffered, he threatened not; but committed himself to him that judgeth righteously" (2:19, 21, 23).

This is a deep discipline of the soul, this evidence of our true sonship with God, as described by our Lord Jesus Christ, "But I say unto you, Love your enemies, bless them that curse you, do good to them that hate you, and pray for them which despitefully use you, and persecute you; That ye may be the children of your Father which is in heaven: for he maketh his sun to rise on the evil and on the good, and sendeth rain on the just and on the unjust" (Matt. 5:44, 45).

David's conduct before Shimei illustrates excellently the discipline endured by those who are defamed (II Sam. 16:5-14). The moment seized upon by the Benjaminite blasphemer of the king could hardly be more excruciatingly cruel. Not only was the king advanced in years, and being driven from his capital city; but all was caused by the rebellion of his own son Absalom, whom he loved dearly. Shimei's stinging insults were being added to Absalom's studied injuries (cf. II Sam. 15:4, "Oh, that I were made judge in the land"). Upon the bleeding heart of an old father was heaped the invective, "Come out, come out, thou bloody man, and thou man of Belial" (16:7), which hurt far more intensely than the stones that were thrown (16:13).

The cursing of Shimei was too caustic for David's mighty men; and Abishai echoed their fierce resentment in his request, "Why should this dead dog curse my lord the king? let me go over, I pray thee, and take off his head" (16:9).

David's response was touching in its expression of tenderness toward a misguided man, and of trust toward Almighty God: "Let him alone, and let him curse . . . It may be that the Lord will look on mine affliction . . . " (16:11, 12). Long before and many times he had faced similar circumstances; and he had learned to commit his cause unto Him that judgeth righteously. In his youth he had lost his temper (justifiably, some of us may think) at the gross ingratitude and invective of Nabal (I Sam. 25: 2-13). In the gracious providence of God he had been restrained and rebuked by the gentle reasonings of Abigail, "That this shall be no grief unto thee, nor offense of heart unto my lord, either that thou hast shed blood causeless, or that my lord hath avenged himself" (25:31). On that occasion he had seen the vindication of God upon his decision not to return evil for evil (25:32-38).

This lesson is written large in his Psalms, to be found on nearly every page, as though we too have need of having this discipline. He had prayed, "Help, Lord, for the godly man ceaseth; for the faithful fail from among the children of men. They speak vanity every one with his neighbor: with flattering lips and with a double heart they speak"; and he had been assured, "For the oppression of the poor, for the sighing of the needy, now will I arise, saith the Lord; I will set him in safety from him that puffeth at him" (Ps. 12:1,2,5). In amazement he had cried out, "False witnesses did rise up; they laid to my charge things that I knew not. They rewarded me evil for good to the spoiling of my soul. But as for me, when they were sick, my clothing was sackcloth: I humbled my soul with fasting . . . I behaved myself as though he had been my friend or brother . . . But in mine adversity they rejoiced, . . . they did tear me, and ceased not" (35:11-15).

He had determined, by God's help, "I will take heed to my ways, that I sin not with my tongue: I will keep my mouth with a bridle, while the wicked is before me" (39:1). He had observed, "I have seen the wicked in great power, and spreading himself like a green bay tree. Yet he passed away, and, lo, he was not: yea, I sought him, but he could not be found" (37:35, 36). He could testify, out of deep and prolonged experience, "Oh how great is thy goodness, which thou hast laid up for them that fear thee; which thou hast wrought for them that trust in thee before the sons of men! Thou shalt hide them in the secret of thy presence from the pride of man: thou shalt keep them secretly in a pavilion from the strife of tongues. Blessed be the Lord: for he hath showed me his marvellous kindness in a strong city" (31:19-21).

It appears from the heading that Psalm 3 was written by David when he fled from Absalom; and it portrays vividly and accurately the thoughts of the king as he went into exile. Although there were many that rose up against him and troubled him (vs. 1), he could say, "But thou, O Lord, art a shield for me; my glory, and the lifter up of mine head" (vs. 3). Of all that rose up against him, Shimei was the most persistent and annoying gad-fly, but graciously the broken-hearted David could declare, "Let him alone, and let him curse."

David is not alone in his submission to savage and searching invective, and this to show that "a soft answer turneth away wrath" (Prov. 15:1). Moses, in his day the meekest of men, suffered cursing and contumely, not only from the multitude, which could be overlooked, but even from his own brother and sister, on a trumped-up accusation against his wife (Num. 12). Before the violent invective of Korah and his fellow conspirators, there was only the falling upon his face and the committal of the whole matter to God (Num. 17). In both cases the Most High honored the humility of His trusting servant.

The Master Himself, the Lord Jesus Christ, knew this discipline of defamation in supreme measure. Was man ever spoken against more falsely or viciously than the Son of Man? He restored to strength a man's hand that withered, and received only the wrath of the politicians who plotted forthwith to be rid of Him (Mk. 3:1-6). He delivered pitiable human beings from the power of indwelling demons, and was portrayed as possessing demon power himself (3:22-30). For His word of mercy and His deeds of might He received from His fellow citizens of Nazareth a

contemptuous sneer, "Is not this the carpenter?" (6:3).
With a kiss he was betrayed by one of his own followers (14:45). On trial for His life he was accused
by many false witnesses, toward whose perversities
"he held his peace" (14:61). Before Pilate, who had
the power of life and death, He was accused of many
things by the chief priests, the religious leaders of
His people; "but he answered nothing" (15:3,5). In
the days of His flesh He had fulfilled the prophetic
word of Isaiah, "He shall not cry, nor lift up, nor cause
his voice to be heard in the street. A bruised reed
shall he not break, and the smoking flax shall he not
quench: he shall bring forth judgment unto truth"
(Isa. 42:2, 3); and in the shadow of death He fulfilled that further word, "He was oppressed, and he
was afflicted, yet he opened not his mouth: he is
brought as a lamb to the slaughter, and as a sheep
before her shearers is dumb, so he openeth not his
mouth" (53:7). He knew in practice what He had
declared in precept, "Blessed are ye, when men shall
revile you, and persecute you, and shall say all manner
of evil against you falsely, for my sake. Rejoice, and
be exceeding glad: for great is your reward in heaven:
for so persecuted they the prophets which were before
you" (Matt. 5:11, 12).

Paul, the pre-eminent servant of the lowly Saviour,
showed forth the fruits of this discipline. He knew
what it meant to be "troubled on every side, yet not
distressed; ... perplexed, but not in despair; persecuted,
but not forsaken; cast down, but not destroyed"

(II Cor. 4:8, 9). In Macedonia, then as now an area of turmoil, he could say, "We were troubled on every side; without were fightings, within were fears" (7:5). He could declare the just principle of evangelical practice. "Recompense to no man evil for evil. Provide things honest in the sight of all men. If it be possible, as much as lieth in you, live peaceably with all men. Dearly beloved, avenge not yourselves, but rather give place unto wrath: for it is written, Vengeance is mine; I will repay, saith the Lord. Therefore if thine enemy hunger, feed him; if he thirst, give him drink: for in so doing thou shalt heap coals of fire on his head. Be not overcome of evil, but overcome evil with good" (Rom. 12:17-21).

The discipline of defamation, how deeply it digs into our soul; but from the upturned earth there springs the fair flowers of divine fragrance, the graciousness of the Lord Jesus Himself.

Beneath His Banner

'Twixt God and thee but love shall be;
'Twixt earth and thee distrust and fear,
'Twixt sin and thee shall be hate and war;
And hope shall be 'twixt Heaven and thee
    Till night is o'er.
                —Mechthild of Hellfde, A.D. 1277.

THE DISCIPLINE OF
DEFENSE

"And there is none of you that is sorry for me"
(I Sam. 22:8).

THESE ARE the words of a king! Who would have thought it could be so? A sovereign stooping to self-pity, a monarch making himself miserable and mean, a crown that cries like a spoiled child! But that is what the story tells, with penetrating insight and illumination into the character of Saul, first king of Israel.

It would seem that selfishness and self-pity were not conspicuous in Saul's character at the outset of his royal career. On the contrary, there seem to be some characteristics that are unusually commendable. He came of a good family (I Sam. 9:1), and was a dutiful son, "a choice young man, and a goodly: and there was not among the children of Israel a goodlier person than he" (9:2). Tall, handsome, competent, co-operative, he had the qualifications to be captain over God's people (9:16). Withal he was humbled and unassuming. He made no boast to his relatives about the anointing of kingship (10:14-16), and when he was sought of Samuel to be publicly proclaimed as king, "he hath hid himself among the stuff" (10:22). He made no reply to his critics (and what young man raised to any place of responsibility or authority does not have an abundant supply of the scornful); rather, when "they despised him, and brought him no presents . . . he held his peace" (10:27). I like that. It takes strength of character and confidence in God to keep one's tongue when he is derided and despised by the malicious and merciless. They judged him before he had opportunity to prove himself; but he could keep sweet.

When the occasion arose to reveal his qualities of leadership, he was not inadequate (11:4-11); and a signal victory was achieved under his generalship. Again he showed that he could be magnanimous; for when his soldiers wanted to cut off his erstwhile critics, Saul could say with generosity, "There shall not a man be put to death this day: for today the Lord hath wrought salvation in Israel" (11:13). Those are the words of a king!

However, flaws began to appear in his personality and character; qualities that would have to be discarded completely if he were to continue truly a king. Despite his home training (or because of it?), and his anointing with the oil of God at the hand of Samuel, he seemed to lack a sense of the spiritual. He was earthly-minded, despite his language indicating a trust in God. He was self-willed, impulsive and imperious; and when it seemed that Samuel tarried in coming to the troops, Saul presumed the prerogatives of the priest by offering the sacrifice. That presumption may not seem important to us, for we lack the background of the sacrificial ceremonialism of the Jews, and the utter sanctity of the altar and its sacrifice. This low regard of Saul for the things of God made it apparent to Samuel that Saul lacked some basic essentials of kingship (13:13,14).

Saul seemed to lack a sense of fitness in things human as well as divine. When a great victory was in the making, after it had seemed that the cause was hopeless because of the odds against him (13:15-23), the king hampered the efforts of his men rather than helped them by his denying them any food (14:24). Even his own son Jonathan had to admit, "My father hath troubled the land: see, I pray you, how mine eyes have been enlightened, because I tasted a little of this honey. How much more, if haply the people had eaten freely to day of the spoil of their enemies which they found?" (14:29,30). Saul had received some object lessons in things human and divine; and it was up to him to profit thereby. If so, he would still be a king; if not, he was a failure.

The test came some years later in the matter of the Amalekites, the fierce, implacable foes of Israel (15:1-3). His instructions were clear (15:3); his obedience was only partial, for "Saul and the people spared Agag, and the best of the sheep . . . and all that was good . . . but everything that was vile and refuse, that they destroyed utterly" (15:9). The test was made; the failure was obvious; and the Most High revealed to Samuel, "It repenteth me that I have set up Saul to be king: for he is turned back from following me, and hath not performed my commandments" (15:11).

Taken from the people, entrusted with the kingdom, tested in implicit and unquestioning obedience to God, he was found wanting. And what was his excuse? "Yea, I have obeyed the voice of the Lord . . . but the people" (15:20,21). In the earlier incident, when irreverently and impetuously he intruded into the office of the priest, he excused himself in like manner, "Because I saw that the people were scattered . . . the Philistines will come . . . " (13:11,12). The people, the Philistines; always somebody else was at fault! Those were not the words of a true king.

Impetuosity, impatience, petulance, pride, these are not kingly, nor manly characteristics; and because they were not faced squarely and conquered within his own breast, they overcame Saul. He becomes a smaller man as he grows older, picayunish, peevish, pitiful. He revealed his true self in his own words of wailing, "and there is none of you that is sorry for me" (22:8).

This is the discipline of defense. As long as a man is on the aggressive, alert to his liabilities and limitations, active in his service for God and man, he can be courageous, generous, altruistic, large-spirited; but when he allows himself to get on the defensive: defending his position, policies, procedure, personality, program, then he tends to become timid, selfish, self-centered, and small. He has lost the magnanimity that can minimize insults and injuries. He forgets the wholesomeness and soul-health necessary for his own soul, as indicated in a prayer of Phillip Brooks, "Let me not lose faith in my fellow men. Keep me sweet and sound of heart, in spite of ingratitude, treachery or meanness. Preserve me from minding little stings or giving them."

Self-centeredness makes a man soft, sensitive, selfish. Self-pity makes him pitiable, a picture of pathos when he should be a power for good. Self-importance makes him unimpressive, important in his own eyes but impossible to others. Conceit makes him contemptible. Bitterness of spirit over the success of others makes him blind to his own shortcomings. Envy makes him unenviable. Petulance makes him picayunish. Self-pampering makes him sarcastic. Self-indulgence makes him indolent. Self-defense destroys his self-respect, and makes him less a man.

This, I say, is the discipline of defense. To whimper is to be a weakling; to complain is to be coward; to blame others is to be a baby; to pity self is to be pitiful; to yell is to be "yellow," which term of contempt contains the whole concept of the unworthy and worthless.

The discipline of defense demands that we destroy

self-centeredness, self-pity, self-importance, self-indulgence, self-defense of any kind. If others are honored, congratulate them (I Cor. 12:26); if you are neglected, forget it. If the job is too big for you, admit it to yourself and to others and step aside graciously; you will be a bigger and better man for it. If others can do the job better than you, let them do it with your "God bless you!" Let no dog-in-the-manger attitude make you snappy, showing teeth and temper rather than kindness and courtesy; in other words, be a Christian rather than a cur!

The discipline of defense is to "be kindly affectioned one to another with brotherly love; in honor preferring one another . . . not to think of himself more highly than he ought to think; but to think soberly, according as God hath dealt to every man the measure of faith . . . (to) bless them which persecute you; (to) bless and curse not" (Rom. 12:10,3,14). It is to "let nothing be done through strife or vainglory; but in lowliness of mind (to) let each esteem other better than themselves . . . (to) do all things without murmurings and disputings: that ye may be blameless and harmless, the sons of God, without rebuke" (Phil. 2:3,14,15). It is to do your duty and to do good unto others.

To defend yourself is to descend to the despicable, the degrading, the destructive; to deny yourself is to ascend to the worth-while, the wholesome and the helpful. It is to be a man or woman of God, fashioned in the furnace of affliction, tested in the trials of life, living on the plane of perfect submission to the Son of God, who "made himself of no reputation, . . . and became obedient unto death, even the death of the cross. Wherefore God also hath highly exalted him" (Phil. 2:7-9). To bear the cross is to display the royalty of heaven, while to deny the cross is to defend our mean selves; to indulge in self pity is to degrade ourselves, while to play the man's part in the power of the Spirit is to please Him who defended not Himself.

Anywhere with Jesus I can safely go,
Anywhere He leads me in this world below;
Anywhere without Him dearest joys would fade;
Anywhere with Jesus I am not afraid.

Anywhere with Jesus I am not alone;
Other friends may fail me, He is still my own;
Though His hand may lead me over dreary ways,
Anywhere with Jesus is a house of praise.

Art Thou Weary, Art Thou Languid

Art thou weary, art thou languid,
Art thou sore distressed?
"Come to Me," saith One, "and coming
    Be at rest."

Hath He marks to lead me to Him,
If He be my guide?
"In His feet and hands are wound-prints,
    And His side."

Is there diadem, as Monarch,
That His brow adorns?
"Yea, a crown, in very surety;
    But of thorns."

If I find Him, if I follow,
What His guerdon here?
"Many a sorrow, many a labor,
    Many a tear."

If I still hold closely to Him,
What hath He at last?
"Sorrow vanquished, labor ended,
    Jordan passed."

If I ask Him to receive me,
Will He say me nay?
"Not till earth, and not till heaven
    Pass away."

Finding, following, keeping, struggling,
Is He sure to bless?
"Saints, apostles, prophets, martyrs,
    Answer, Yes."

—St. Stephen, the Sabaite, Eighth Century,
    Translated by John M. Neale, 1862.

THE DISCIPLINE OF
DEFORMITY

"The lame take the prey" (Isa. 33:23).

THERE ARE few, if any, disciplines of the soul that sink as deeply into the human spirit as that of physical deformity. Doubt, discouragement, defamation, desperation, even disease does not dig so deeply into the inner heart as does bodily handicap. Frustration and fear follow it, so that life itself seems mad folly and utter futility; while the Most High, in His infinite tenderness and mercy says, "Strengthen ye the weak hands, and confirm the feeble knees. Say to them that are of a fearful heart, Be strong, fear not: behold, your God will come with vengeance, even God with a recompence; he will come and save you. Then the eyes of the blind shall be opened, and the ears of the deaf shall be unstopped. Then shall the lame man leap as an hart, and the tongue of the dumb sing: for in the wilderness shall waters break out, and streams in the desert" (Isa. 35:3-6).

One remembers Lord Byron's bitterness of soul over his physical handicap, as he said,

"My poor mother was generally in a rage every

day, and used to render me sometimes almost frantic; particularly when, in her passion, she reproached me with my personal deformity, I have left her presence to rush into solitude, where, unseen, I could vent the rage and mortification I endured, and curse the deformity, that I now began to consider as a signal work of the injustice of Providence. Those were bitter moments; even now, the impression of them is vivid in my mind; and they cankered a heart that I believe was naturally affectionate, and destroyed a temper always disposed to be violent. It was my feeling at this period that suggested the idea of 'The Deformed Transformed.' I often look back on the days of my childhood, and am astonished at the recollection of the intensity of my feelings at that period;—the first impressions are indelible. My poor mother, and after her my school-feilows by their taunts, had led me to consider my lameness as the greatest misfortune, and I have never been able to conquer this feeling. It requires great natural goodness of disposition, as well as reflection, to conquer the corroding bitterness that deformity engenders in the mind, and which, while preying on itself, sours one toward all the world. I have read, that where personal deformity exists, it may be always traced in the face, however handsome the face may be. I am sure that what is meant by this is, that the consciousness of it gives to the countenance an habitual expression of discontent, which I believe is the case; yet it is too bad (added Byron with bitter-

ness) that, because one had a defective foot, one cannot have a perfect form."[1]

One sits beside Byron in sorrow of spirit, for one
would fain have him turn from the introspection and
introversion of the "corroding bitterness ... which
while preying on itself, sours one toward all the world"
to the assurance and uplift of Isaiah's promise, "The
lame shall take the prey." If he, and thousands with
him, could only hearken to the testimony of one who
had an unspeakably cruel "thorn" in his flesh the
nature of which is nowhere revealed, from which
"thorn" he prayed earnestly to be delivered, but without avail. He learned, however, and would teach Lord
Byron if he could, that there is a delight higher than
deliverance; for he learned from the Lord Jesus Christ,
that, "My grace is sufficient for thee: for my strength
is made perfect in weakness" (II Cor. 12:9). Therefore he could say with inner exultation, "Most gladly
therefore will I rather glory in my infirmities, that
the power of Christ may rest upon me. Therefore
I take pleasure in infirmities, in reproaches, in necessities, in persecutions, in distresses for Christ's sake:
for when I am weak, then am I strong" (II Cor. 12:9,
10).

Grace that is sufficient, strength made perfect in
weakness, pleasure in infirmities, strength when I am
weak, that the power of Christ may rest upon me:

---

[1] Countess of Blessington, *A Journal of Conversation with Lord Byron*,
(Boston: William Veazie, 1859), pp. 143, 144.

this is the discipline of deformity. This is the triumph over the thorn, the song over the suffering, the rejoicing over reproach, the glorying in grace, the defeat of deformity.

The lame have access to the king, and are the special object of his solicitude. Is there story lovelier than that of David's desire to help the sons of Jonathan, because of the heart covenant he had made with the companion of his youth (I Sam. 20: 14-16; 23:18; II Sam. 21:7)! He found that there remained one son of Jonathan, Mephibosheth by name, "which is lame on his feet" (II Sam. 9:3). For the lame there was love, thoughtfulness, tenderness, care and provision, even privilege to eat at the king's table. "So Mephibosheth dwelt in Jerusalem: for he did eat continually at the king's table; and was lame on both feet" (9:13). Handicapped, but a special home in the court; infirm, but on intimate terms with his Majesty; lame, but loved by David; deformed, but dining with the king. And has the Lord of Glory, David's greater Son, less compassion for the crippled?

The leper has service for his king. Outside the pale of his people, "unclean" by highest judgment, unwanted by fellow humans, the leper seemed a burden to himself and a bane to others. Yet it was the leper whom God sent to show that the enemy had fled, that food had become available in abundance to the storming multitudes of Samaria, as he had promised through his servant Elisha (II Kings 7). The promise, "Tomorrow about this time shall a measure of fine flour be sold for a shekel, ... in the gate of Samaria" seemed so preposterous that a minister of state remonstrated, "Behold, if the Lord would make windows in heaven, might this thing be?" (vss. 1,2).

The Almighty does have "windows in heaven" (Mal. 3:10), from which to pour blessings upon His needy children; but He delights in using the useless, in dispatching the deformed, to open them. The four lepers in the story led their king and country to the accomplishment of God's promise. The inconspicuous have their inning, the incompetent make their contribution, the unsightly serve their God and fellow men, and the handicapped help open windows in heaven!

Bunyan has a tender t o u c h for the tested and troubled ones who feel that their infirmity renders them insufficient to be of any service whatever. Greatheart and his courageous companions such as Mr. Honest, Christiana and her four stalwart sons, Mercy, and others were on their way to the City of The Great King, where they met Mr. Feeble-mind, who "made as if he intended to linger." (By Mr. Feeblemind Bunyan did not intend one who was mentally incompetent, but one that was "weak in the faith.") He was hesitant to accompany such accomplished pilgrims, and sought to beg off, saying, "Alas! I want a suitable companion. You are all lusty and strong, but I, as you see, am weak ... by reason of my many infirmities, I should be a burden to myself and to you

... Nay, I am so weak as to be offended with that which others have a liberty to do. I do not yet know all the truth; I am a very ignorant Christian man... It is with me as it is with a weak man among the strong, or as with a sick man among the healthy, or as a lamp despised."

In the midst of their discussion, "Mr. Ready-to-halt came by, with his crutches in his hands; and also was going on a pilgrimage." To him spoke the weak Christian, "I was but now complaining that I had not a suitable companion, but thou art according to my wish"; to which Mr. Ready-to-halt replied with gracious spirit and offered him one of his crutches.

And who can have more compassion on the weak than have the crippled, or more heart for the helpless than the handicapped?

Not only God's "lame ones" and "lepers" can bring love and lilt of laughter to others, but his blind ones can cause them to see glories hitherto hidden. Is there a Christian heart unmoved by the message of that hymn, "O, Love That Will Not Let Me Go," especially when it remembers that its author was blind? The late Rev. George Matheson, D.D., of Edinburgh was blind; yet he could see the wonders of God's love, and point others to them. With a heart overflowing with faith he could say to his fellow-handicapped, and to all of us:

"My soul, it was by the gate of the temple called

Beautiful that the lame man was laid; in the moments of thine impotence, remember that. Remember that thine experience of the cross is itself the gate into the temple of sympathy. I do not say it is thine only gate into *Heaven;* Heaven has many temples—many mansions. Thou shalt know by training here what shall be thy temple yonder. Perhaps thine is here an inquiring mind; there are yonder those who inquire in His temple! Perhaps thine is here the gift of eloquence; there are yonder those who in His temple speak of His glory. Perhaps thou hast here the spirit of an artist; there are yonder those whose temple is a place in which to behold the beauty of the Lord. But it may be that here thy lot is simply to lie low—to be prostrated on a bed of pain. That battered gate is the most beautiful of all. It is thy training for the right service. It is thy school for learning the art of mercy. The barrier that chains thee is a rudimentary wing; one day thou shalt fly with it."[2]

Seeing in the shadow of blindness, singing in the sadness of sorrow, serving in the loneliness of lameness, strengthened in the grace that is sufficient: this is the discipline of deformity, that makes sweet our spirit, and strengthens that of others.

---

[2] George Matheson, *Thoughts for Life's Journeys,* (London: James Clarke & Co., 1907), pp. 150, 151.

Say not my soul, "from whence
    Can God relieve my care?"
Remember that Omnipotence
    Hath servants everywhere.

His help is always sure,
    His methods seldom guessed;
Delay will make our pleasure pure;
    Surprise will give it zest.

His wisdom is sublime,
    His heart profoundly kind;
God never is before His time,
    And never is behind.

Hast thou assumed a load
    Which none will bear with thee?
And art thou bearing it for God,
    And shall He fail to see?

—J. J. Lynch

THE DISCIPLINE OF
DELAY

"For ye have need of patience" (*Heb.* 10:36).

W E HAVE been told that God's disappointments are His appointments, that God's delays are not His denials; but do we believe what we hear? Delay, with its apparent destruction of all hope, can be a deep discipline to the soul that would serve the Lord Jesus. We live in a restless, impatient day. We have little time for preparation, and less for meditation or worship. We feel we must be active, energetic, enthusiastic, and humanly effective; and we cannot understand why inactivity, weakness, weariness, and seeming uselessness should become our lot. It all appears to be so futile and foolish, without plan or purpose.

The discipline of delay is written large in the life of God's people, as we could observe in Abraham's long waiting for the son of promise, in Joseph's years in Egypt as victim of cruel circumstances, in Moses' long obscurity in the desert, in Hannah's empty home and aching heart, even in the silent years spent by our Lord Jesus in the narrow streets of Nazareth.

We trace that discipline in a few lives whose experience we can compare with our own, for our learning and encouragement.

David knew this discipline. As a lad, caring for his father's sheep, he was anointed of Samuel to be king over Israel; but thereafter stretched years of delay, on the stony hillsides of Bethlehem, in the cave of Adullam whither he had been driven by in the insane and unnecessary envy of Saul, until he fled to the fierce Philistines, more friendly than his own people. There he could say truly, "I was a reproach among all mine enemies, but especially among my neighbors, and a fear to mine acquaintance: they that did see me without fled from me. I am forgotten as a dead man out of mind: I am like a broken vessel" (Ps. 31:11,12). The delay seemed to be interminable and intolerable, but was indispensable in preparing David for his long career as king of his people, to which office he had been appointed many years before. Delay never thwarts God's purpose; rather, it polishes His instrument.

Elijah endured the exercise of patience. Called to prophetic office in a day of moral and spiritual declension among his people, he announced the judgment of famine with all the vigor of pyrotechnic personality. At the moment when it seemed he was most needed by his people, he experienced an inexplicable, inscrutable delay, with "Get thee hence, and turn thee eastward, and hide thyself by the brook

Cherith" (I Kings 17:3). Israel's famine for bread and the Word of God burned deeply into his soul; their lack of repentance grieved him; his solitary position of obedience toward God and the solitude of his lonely post seemed overwhelming. Even the brook, with its friendly murmuring and its supply of needed water, dried up. The discipline was not yet complete, for there remained silent years in a humble home in Zarephath, among strangers and aliens. When God's hour came, however, the discipline of Cherith and Zarephath was distilled into intercession on Mount Carmel that brought heavenly fire upon the altar and rain upon the thirsty fields. Delay does not forget God's servants nor cause His faithfulness to fail; rather, it fortifies their souls and vindicates His name.

Paul came to know the patience of hindered purpose. Stopped at the gate of Damascus, penitent in the street called Straight, seeing under the touch of Ananias and filled with the Spirit he was a chosen vessel to bear the gospel to great and small. "Straightway he preached Christ in the synagogues, that he is the Son of God" (Acts 9:20). Then came the discipline of delay in the desert of Arabia, where he learned by revelation of God, not by precept of man, the glorious gospel of the grace of God. From Arabia he could go to Antioch and its world-wide missionary program, to Athens and its proud Areopagus, to Achaia and its wicked Corinth, to the arena of Ephesus, and if necessary, to Rome. The delay that instructs and prepares saves time, never loses it. From it one can walk with a step of assurance and a heart of flame.

Hudson Taylor knew the testing that tempers the steel of the soul. Invalided, home at twenty-nine after six years of intensive service in China, he settled with his little family in the east end of London. Outside interests lessened; friends began to forget; and five long hidden years were spent in the dreary street of a poor part of London, where the Taylors were "shut up to prayer and patience." From the record of those years it has been written, "Yet, without those hidden years, with all their growth and testing, how could the vision and enthusiasm of youth have been matured for the leadership that was to be?" Faith, faithfulness, devotion, self-sacrifice, unremitting labor, patient, persevering prayer became their portion and power, but more, there is "the deep, prolonged exercise of a soul that is following hard after God . . . the gradual strengthening here, of a man called to walk by faith not by sight; the unutterable confidence of a heart cleaving to God and God alone, which pleases Him as nothing else can."[1] As the years of obscurity progressed, "prayer was the only way by which the burdened heart could obtain any relief"; and when the discipline was complete, there emerged the China Inland Mission, at first only a tiny root, but destined of God to fill the land of China with gospel fruit.

---

[1] Dr. and Mrs. Howard Taylor *Hudson Taylor's Spiritual Secret.* China Inland Mission. (London, Philadelphia and Toronto: 1935), pp. 75, 76.

Have you come to the discipline of delay? Inactivity you have for activity, weakness for strength, silence for speaking, sickness for health, forgetfulness for friendship, obscurity for opportunity. Let the darkness of delay discipline your soul in the patience of the saints, in the promises of God, who will not suffer His faithfulness to fail, in the presence of the Saviour by His Spirit, in the provision of needed grace from nail-scarred Hands. In God's time and way there will be position for you as for David, prevailing prayer as for Elijah, and place of service as for Paul, and Hudson Taylor. Delay will strengthen and hasten your steps of true service.

In every life
There's a pause that is better than onward rush,
Better than hewing or mightiest doing;
'Tis the standing still at Sovereign will.

There's a hush that is better than ardent speech,
Better than sighing or wilderness crying;
'Tis the being still at Sovereign will.

The pause and the hush sing a double song
In unison low and for all time long.
O human soul, God's working plan
Goes on, nor needs the aid of man!
   Stand still, and see!
   Be still, and know!

Thankfulness

My God, I thank Thee who hast made
    The Earth so bright;
So full of splendour and of joy,
    Beauty and light;
So many glorious things are here,
    Noble and right!

I thank Thee, too, that Thou hast made
    Joy to abound;
So many gentle thoughts and deeds
    Circling us round,
That in the darkest spot of Earth
    Some love is found.

.   .   .   .

I thank Thee, Lord, that Thou hast kept
    The best in store;
We have enough, yet not too much
    To long for more:
A yearning for a deeper peace,
    Not known before.

I thank Thee, Lord, that here our souls,
    Though amply blest,
Can never find, although they seek,
    A perfect rest
Nor ever shall, until they lean
    On Jesus' breast!

                    —Adelaide A. Procter.*

*From POEMS by Adelaide A. Procter. Used by permission of the publishers, Nimmo, Hay & Mitchell, Edinburgh.

THE DISCIPLINE OF
DELIGHT

"I know how to abound" (*Phil.* 4:12).

Some people seem to get all the good things in life; and to our way of thinking we get quite the reverse. They seem to have abundance of resources, and all that goes with money, clothes, car, companions, ease, and education, while we plod along, quite penniless; theirs, abundance of health in energy, endurance, athletic ability, and good looks, while we carry weary body and aching heart. They have prosperity and prominence, poise and position, friends and favor, family and affection home and hospitality; in the words of the Psalmist, "They have more than heart could wish" (Ps. 73:7).

Pride is a great enemy of the soul; and Scripture has much to say on that point. "When pride cometh, then cometh shame" (Prov. 11:2). "Only by pride cometh contention" (13:10). "Pride goeth before destruction, and a haughty spirit before a fall" (16:18). "Seest thou a man wise in his own conceit? there is more hope of a fool than of him" (26:12). "A man's pride shall bring him low" (29:23); and above all, "God resisteth the proud, and giveth grace to the humble. Humble yourselves therefore under the mighty hand of God" (I Pet. 5:5,6).

The discipline of delight humbles the haughty heart, sweetens the spirit, mellows the brimming mind, and chastens the churlish temper. Self-sufficiency and sophistication are distilled by this discipline into the sweetness that says, "Not that we are sufficient: to think any thing as of ourselves; but our sufficiency is of God" (II Cor. 3:5).

The career of Moses illustrates excellently this discipline of delight. By native endowment he had everything one might covet; but he gave all away that he might have heavenly enduement for a worthwhile task. Justifiably, he might have been proud, for from babyhood he was very handsome. (His parents saw he was a "proper," a beautiful child, Heb. 11:23; "exceeding fair," Acts 7:20; "a goodly child," Exod. 2:2). "Face value" is often in contrast to "real value," whether we think in terms of economics or of character; because for some, fair features create a "pride of face" that shrivels the soul and makes it ugly. A good face and a good heart go together; a pretty face may presume to itself prerogatives that its heart does not possess. Withal, handsome Moses became the humblest of men, unlike many others who could endure no humbling of heart.

Moses also might have had "pride of place." He was recognized as belonging to royalty, "the son of Pharaoh's daughter" (Heb. 11:24; Exod. 2:10; Acts

7:21). An adopted son often assumes airs that a real son would disdain. We might expect Moses to lord it over his lowly fellows, as would any small soul raised to such dizzy prominence; but on the contrary, "he went out unto his brethren, and looked on their burdens" (Exod. 2:11). Place had not made him proud.

Nor had learning! Because of place he had opportunity for education in a day when very few were even literate. "Moses was learned in all the wisdom of the Egyptians" (Acts 7:22). "A little learning is a dangerous thing," and it seems that many become silly or ridiculous when they strut their meager achievement. They seem educated beyond their intelligence. Their language resounds with pompous polysyllables in place of plain Anglo-Saxon words; their manner is marked by condescension toward the less-informed rather than by meekness of wisdom as was the Apostle Paul. He, like Moses, had understanding of the deep mysteries of God, yet he came not with "excellency of speech" or "enticing words of man's wisdom" (I Cor. 2:1-4). Learning had not made him proud.

Nor had achievement! Moses was "mighty in words and in deeds" (Acts 7:22). Tradition has it that he became commander-in-chief of the armies of Egypt; and his leadership of the unruly children of Israel in the wilderness revealed the organization and discipline that came from military training. Accomplishment makes some people proud, be their product large or small. "Is not this great Babylon, that I have built?" said Nebuchadnezzar before pride removed his reason; and he was seven years in learning to "honor the King of heaven, all whose works are truth, and his ways judgment" (Dan. 4:30, 37). Mighty deeds make some men mad, as though achievement had set them apart from other toilers; and they become impatient or overbearing in their attitudes. Not so with Moses, for the discipline of delight made him "very meek, above all the men which were upon the face of the earth" (Num. 12:3).

Looks and books, society and industry, these and a thousand other factors make for some of us "the pride of life"; and only by drastic disciplining of ourselves can we be useful for God and for our fellow men. Moses points out the pathway to that service. Rather than delight in himself and his distinctions he concerned himself with the difficulties of others. "It came into his heart to visit his brethren" (Acts 7:23). Unselfish interest in the welfare of others makes us unconcerned about any natural gifts and graces we may have. We forget ourselves in helping others; and others are then conscious, not of our person and position, but rather of the Christ who dwells in our hearts.

Choosing to suffer affliction for others becomes a genuine delight to us (Heb. 11:25). We identify ourselves with a Cause that is humanly unpopular, but which has the approval of Heaven. We renounce our rights in order to be on the right side; and a title to which we are entitled (as "the son of Pharaoh's daughter" belonged to Moses) becomes a mere trifle, if only we be known as "the sons of God." The portion belonging to God's people is far more important to us than the "pleasures of sin for a season" (Heb. 11:25); to be reproached for the Cause of Christ, to bear His Name, to us exceeds the choicest treasures of earth (Heb. 11:26; I Pet. 4:14). We depend not upon our knowledge nor ability; rather we also "endure as seeing him who is invisible" (Heb. 11:27).

There is satisfaction in serving the Lord Jesus; sweetness in suffering for His Name; blessing in bearing His reproach; pleasure in becoming a pilgrim; delight in doing His bidding. To have every natural delight: face, form, education, erudition, personality, position, achievement, and acclaim of others is to need the discipline of delight, that every gift be acknowledged as from the Giver, that every talent become a sacred trust, that every honor become a humbling of heart before Him, in order that He have all the glory. Then, like Moses of old, with lowly heart and veiled face, we shall walk where He leads, shall be thankful for daily manna, shall endure as seeing Him who is invisible, shall believe Him when every other friend fails. Then comes to pass the word, "Delight thyself also in the Lord, and he shall give thee the desires of thine heart" (Ps. 37:4).

No Scar?

Hast thou no scar?
No hidden scar on foot, or side, or hand?
I hear thee sung as mighty in the land,
I hear them hail thy bright ascendant star,
Hast thou no scar?

Hast thou no wound?
Yet I was wounded by the archers, spent,
Leaned Me against a tree to die; and rent
By ravening wolves that compassed me, I swooned:
Hast thou no wound?

No wound? no scar?
Yet, as the Master shall the servant be,
And pierced are the feet that follow Me;
But thine are whole: can he have followed far
Who hath no wound nor scar?

—Amy Carmichael.*

*From TOWARD JERUSALEM by Amy Carmichael. Used by permission of the publishers, Society for Promotion of Christian Knowledge, London.

THE DISCIPLINE OF
DEPENDABILITY

"It is good for a man that he bear the yoke in his youth"
(Lam. 3:27).

THE STRENGTH, or weakness, of mature years, is determined largely in the days of youth. The dependability or irresponsibility, the sturdiness or vacillation of character, the sunshine or shadow of personality, the strength or weakness of body, are dependent to a very considerable degree upon what we do, refrain from doing, in the relatively carefree and formative Springtime of our life. God needs strong men and women, who can bear heavy burdens in dark and difficult days; and they can do so, if they have borne the yoke in their youth.

To be unaccustomed to the dependable performance of duties, sometimes perhaps irksome and monotonous, is to be unprepared for the stern realities of life and the stirring service of God. It is no kindness to us that we are allowed to idle away our time, to trifle with our tasks, to quit when we are so minded, to neglect the knowledge of the eternal Word of God and the knowledge of the ages, to work below the level of our ability so that we are satisfied with the mediocre, and to grow up irresponsible, irritable, and immature.

To bear the yoke in one's youth is to become accustomed early to do with cheerfulness one's share of duties, however small that may be at first, to complete one's assignment conscientiously and thoroughly, even though no one sees us, to profit by one's mistakes and to take correction gratefully, to serve for the love of service rather than for reward. To bear the yoke in youth is to be able to bear burdens in later years, and to bring glory thereby unto God.

David, the shepherd boy of Bethlehem who became the king of Israel, illustrates admirably the discipline of dependability. He is not alone in this regard, for we could consider with similar profit the preparatory period of Joseph, Moses, Joshua, Samuel, Esther, or Paul, to mention only a few but David serves our purpose well.

He had the great *fundamental,* the basic essential of any useful and effective life, i.e., a heart that loved God. The Almighty had put Saul, the first king of Israel, to the test, and found him to be lacking in the necessary qualifications of dependability and endurance under strain; and had said, "The Lord hath sought him a man after his own heart, . . . to be captain over his people, because thou hast not kept that which the Lord commanded thee" (I Sam. 13:14). On a later occasion it was said to Saul, "Hath the Lord as great delight in burnt offerings and sacrifices, as in obeying the voice of the Lord? Behold, to obey is better than sacrifice, . . . For rebellion is as the sin of witchcraft, and stubbornness is as iniquity and idolatry"

(I Sam. 15:22,23). Saul's heart was self-centered and selfish, and the course of his whole life determined thereby.

David was "a man after God's own heart" (Ps. 89:20; Acts 13:22). When Samuel, the Judge of Israel, was sent to Bethlehem to anoint one of Jesse's sons to be the next king of the realm, he was impressed very favorably by the appearance and bearing of Eliab, David's oldest brother, and said, "Surely the Lord's anointed is before him" (I Sam. 16:6). The Lord's reply to His servant is very significant, "Look not on his countenance, or on the height of his stature; because I have refused him: for the Lord seeth not as man seeth; for man looketh on the outward appearance, but the Lord looketh on the heart" (16:7). We are impressed by good looks, tall stature, gracious manners, and these are valuable to have; but they are no substitute for a heart that loves God. Not until David, the youngest of eight brothers, stood before Samuel was it said by the Lord, "Arise, anoint him: for this is he" (16:12).

The "heart" is the great fundamental; for it is we ourselves, what we really are. Because our natural heart is sinful (Matt. 15:19), provision is made for us, in that, "A new heart also will I give you, and a new spirit will I put within you: and I will take away the stony heart out of your flesh, and I will give you an heart of flesh. And I will put my spirit within you, and cause you to walk in my statutes . . ." (Ezek. 36:26, 27). It is the pure in heart that see God (Matt. 5:8).

93

It is "with the heart that man believeth unto righteousness" (Rom. 10:10). We are told to "keep thy heart with all diligence; for out of it are the issues of life" (Prov. 4:23). A new heart, good, genuine and gracious is the *sine qua non* of the happy and effective life.

Not all young people know their future so clearly as did David (I Sam. 16:13). However dimly he may have perceived the intent of Samuel's visit and the contrast of the anointing ceremony, he was conscious that in some way, at a distant day, he would become king of his people. Some young men and women learn early in life what they should do with their life: Joseph knew he was called to be a statesman (Gen. 37:5-11); Joshua, to be a military leader (Num. 27:18-23); John, to be a forerunner for the Lord Jesus (Luke 1:76,77; John 1:22,23). Others did not learn until late in life (but in plenty of time for their real service): Moses at the burning bush (Exod. 3:1-10), Simon Peter on the beach of Bethsaida (Luke 5:1-11), Saul of Tarsus at the Damascus gate (Acts 9:1-6).

How many of life's problems and perplexities would be solved for young people if they just knew what the Most High would have them to be. They envy secretly those who are definite in the design of life's pattern: the ministry, the mission field, teaching, nursing, the professions, farming; for they do not know the mind of the Lord that clearly.

What plans should they make? What major should they elect in college? What electives should they choose? What employment should they seek in the summer, as a part of preparation for life? Whether they know their life's calling or not, the most important consideration about the future is to do faithfully what is before them today, for the discipline of dependability demands tasks thoroughly done. Doing their duty today will not leave them in darkness indefinitely. The light will come! (Psalm 112:4; Job 22:28; 23:8-12). Faithfulness leads to fulfillment of dreams, not futility; dependability, to delight of duty.

David was *faithful* in the tasks assigned to him, and in the extra opportunities which were available. He was required to care for his father's sheep, a menial and uninspiring routine. He practised on his harp upon his own initiative; and he applied himself with good zeal to both opportunities. We know something of his faithfulness to his father in his *fearlessness* of the lion and bear that attacked his flock (I Sam. 17: 34, 35). We need more of that devotion in the duties assigned to children and young people, devotion that will stick to the job despite lions of laziness and bears of boredom. Loyalty to parents and employers, at the risk of loss to ourselves, leads to gain over Goliaths in the large conflicts of later life (I Sam. 17:36-51).

It was his attention to the unrequired, the extra-curricular avocation of playing a harp that startles us out of our complacency. He could have contented himself with a passing effort to acquire an indefinite acquaintanceship with a few chords. On the contrary, he learned to play "well" (I Sam. 16:17,18). Perhaps the other shepherd boys derided him for the long hours of practice necessary to mastery of his instrument; and, perhaps they were secretly envious of his skill? However that may be, the hour came that the king needed a skillful harpist; and the shepherd of Bethlehem was that boy.

One of the greatest defeats in the modern training of youth is that accomplishment is not stressed sufficiently. Our lads and lassies study after a fashion, know some arithmetic but not the multiplication tables, play an instrument only passably, read occasionally and write indifferently, work passively without inquisitiveness into what they are doing or imagination as to how they could be more effective. They can do most things "just a little," but nothing "well." The world is looking for the man or woman who can do at least one thing, and be a master of it.

Not infrequently today there is repeated the experience of David in that the mastery of one accomplishment made an open door to wider service. The king needed a *good* harpist! Who would have thought that the painstaking practice on a harp before a few sheep in the wilderness would lead to the court of a king? One remembers a young woman that dusted the office *well*, which accomplishment led to confidence that she would make a good counsellor for a children's camp, which opportunity in turn led to the mission field. Faithfulness in a routine duty of dusting a desk led to far-reaching horizons in Africa! Another college student washed dishes cheerfully and carefully, which brought opportunity for part-time employment in an administrative office, which door opened into wider spheres of service. From careful work, well done, in the kitchen, to a place of large responsibility in Christian service, teaches one the obvious lesson, "Do *well* whatever you are doing!" Be an expert in at least one capacity. The discipline of doing one thing well will develop dependability in every other endeavor.

The discipline of dependability is characterized also by adaptability of the young heart to its circumstances. David had been faithful in caring for his sheep, and in learning to play the harp; and had been promoted to the court of the king (16:21). After a time his services there were no longer needed, and he "returned from Saul to feed his father's sheep at Bethlehem" (17:15). Not every lad can adapt himself so easily from the glamour of the great to the dull detail of duties at home. A touch of prominence and usefulness seems to disqualify some young people for the dishpan or the dusting, the chores, or the church. They forget that distinction and dignity are consonant with dependability in details. Prominence had not made David proud, nor had authority made him arrogant. With graciousness and cheerfulness he could lay aside the clothes of the court and be a shepherd boy again.

Toward the end of the discipline days of youth David became a soldier in the service of Saul; and because of his ability soon became subject to one of the deepest testings of dependability. He was a natural leader of men, "accepted in the sight of all the people"

(18:5). In combat courageous, in camp considerate; in danger daring, in duty dependable, David lived close to his men, and deserved their confidence. He could not help the fact that the throngs ascribed greater success to him than to King Saul (18:6,7). The inevitable result was the unseemly and insane envy of the king, who "eyed David from that day and forward" (18:9).

Envy is always unspeakably cruel and especially so to young people. Because of envy Abel was slain by Cain (Gen. 4:1-8), Joseph was sold as a slave by his elder brothers (Gen. 37:18-28), Moses was resisted by the elders of Israel (Num. 16:3; Ps. 106:16), and the Lord Jesus was delivered to death (Mk. 15:10). The wisest of men said "a sound heart is the life of the flesh: but envy the rottenness of the bones . . . Wrath is cruel, and anger is outrageous; but who is able to stand before envy?" (Prov. 14:30; 27:4).

David, and young hearts like him all down the ages, have been bewildered and bruised by envy. He was just a soldier, obedient, humble, prudent and successful (I Sam. 18:5), and his only response to the king's jaundiced jealousy was wise behavior (18:14). Finally he was compelled to flee for his life (19:10, 18; 20:1, etc.). When there was opportunity for vengeance, he would not lift his hand against his unworthy master (24:1-7; 26:7-11). David committed his cause to the Most High, and said, "The Lord render to every man his righteousness and faithfulness: for the Lord delivered thee into my hand today, but I would not stretch forth mine against the Lord's anointed" (I Sam. 26:23).

Envy on the part of older people is quite possibly the deepest discipline of dependability for young people. Will they remain sweet, unsophisticated, unspoiled when subjected to the murderous malice of those whose places they are destined to assume? Can they, like David, commit their course to God, and not fight back, nor be discouraged? If not, they will be useless to assume large responsibilities in days to come; but if they do, there is no limit to the horizons of God's glad service.

The foundation of a heart that loves God; the confidence of a future that is in His hands; the faithfulness in duty, even to fearlessness before dangers, in associations, and in the fiery trial of envy by elders; these are fundamentals in the deep discipline of dependability. Because of bearing that yoke in youth every young heart exercised thereby will be able in later life, as a true man or woman of God, to bear the heat and burden of each day.

Choose Thou For Me

I dare not choose my lot;
I would not if I might;
Choose Thou for me, my God,
So shall I walk aright.

The kingdom that I seek
Is Thine; so let the way
That leads to it be Thine,
Else surely I might stray.

Take Thou my cup, and it
With joy or sorrow fill;
As best to Thee may seem,
Choose Thou my good and ill.

Choose Thou for me my friends,
My sickness or my health;
Choose Thou my cares for me,
My poverty or wealth.

Not mine—not mine the choice,
In things or great or small;
Be Thou my Guide, my Strength,
My Wisdom and my All!

—Horatius Bonar.

THE DISCIPLINE OF
DESIRE

"For even Christ pleased not himself" (Rom. 15:3).

As a CHRISTIAN, a believer in the Lord Jesus Christ as my personal Saviour, a follower of the Altogether Lovely One, what criteria of Christian conduct should be mine? Should I go to the movies, the theatre, the opera, taverns, Sunday baseball games, and the like? On many points there is a wide variety of opinion, with the warmth of the argument varying in direct proportion to the debatability of the problem.

It appears that the Scriptures distinguish between various types of conduct. Some matters are clearly required: to love the Lord our God with all our heart (Deut. 6:5), to keep His commandments (Exod. 20:1-17, with the understanding that in the New Testament the "Lord's Day," the first day of the week, replaces the Sabbath of Israel), to be kind one to another (Rom. 12:10), to be diligent in our duties (vs.11), to rejoice in hope (vs.12), and others too numerous to mention here. On the other hand there are many things we must avoid because of their being sinful and harmful as in the Decalogue, and elaborated in the Epistles, as "Let him that stole steal no more. . . . Let all bitterness . . . and evil speaking, be put away. . . . But fornication, and all uncleanness, or covetousness, let it not be once named among you. . . . Neither filthiness, nor foolish talking, nor jesting. . . ." "Children, obey your parents: for this is right" (Eph. 4:28—5:4; 6:1), and the like. (See Col. 3).

In between what we are told clearly to do, and what not to do, there is a wide area of border-line cases; matters intrinsically innocent in themselves, but good or evil according to principles found in the Word of God. It is this area that provides most of the confusion for us, and to which we should pay the closest attention, in order that we be consistent and effective Christians.

For those border-line cases the Scriptures give us basic principles of conduct, rather then precepts (Rom. 12-14; I Cor. 8, and elsewhere); and we should catch the spirit as well as the letter of the Word to apply to our conduct. In so doing we must remember that customs and conventions vary from one country to another, as well as from one century to another. The relatively large amount of freedom allowed to American young people would be a stumbling-block to Latin American or Chinese Christians, for example.

The criteria of Christian conduct seem to be the following:

1. There should be no *conformity* to the world (Rom. 12:1,2). What is the world, and worldliness? The Word says, "Love not the world, neither the things that are in the world. If any man love the world, the love of the Father is not in him. For all that is in the world, the lust of the flesh, the lust of the eyes, and the pride of life, is not of the Father, but is of the world. And the world passeth away, and the lust thereof: but he that doeth the will of God abideth forever" (I John 2:15-17). The "world" is a spirit, and is expressed in things. It defies exact definition, because it is a spirit. The closest working definition I have found is that of John Wesley, "Whatever cools my affection toward Christ is the world." This is a subjective standard, to be sure, to be applied individually by each Christian. What may cool my affection for Christ may be a matter of total indifference to you: worldly for me, and not for you! We should ask ourselves the question, however, "Is it conformed to the world?"

2. There should be no *condemnatory* attitude on our part (Rom. 14:1-3). "Let not him that eateth despise him that eateth not; and let not him which eateth not judge him that eateth" (vs.3), for God had approved both of them. The Apostle Paul is using an illustration of worldliness familiar in his day: i.e., should a Christian eat food offered to idols (see I Cor. 10). The idol was nothing in itself; and a Christian could eat or not, according to his own conscience;

but he was not to condemn his fellow Christian of different practice.

3. We are to have our own *convictions*, based upon the Word of God (Rom. 14:4-9). "Let every man be fully persuaded in his own mind" (vs. 5). We are to have the Lord pre-eminent in our lives, to judge ourselves, and not the servant of another (vs. 4). I recall the conversation of long ago with a distinguished servant of Christ. I had proposed to take off a Saturday afternoon (in my college days) to see a football game. He said, "Go ahead; but not I, thank you." He went on to explain that he had been a great sports enthusiast in Canada, and that the Lord had pointed out to him that football on Saturday and preaching on Sunday might be inconsistent (for him). I respected his convictions, and he did not try to change mine on that point.

4. We are to be *considerate* one of another (Rom. 14:10-13). "Let us not therefore judge one another any more: but judge this rather, that no man put a stumbling-block or an occasion to fall in his brother's way" (vs. 13). The matter under consideration may be of itself innocent enough ("nothing [meaning meat here] unclean of itself," vs. 14); but our practice may prove to be a stumbling-block to another. For example, we are told of an immigrant lad from Central Europe that was led to Christ in this country. He was invited to Sunday dinner with an elder in that church; and beer was served. The new convert declined to drink, because by beer he had been led to

strong drink. His host explained that beer with meals was the custom in the old country, and could be in America also. The young Christian bowed to superior knowledge of his elder brother in Christ. On the next Saturday night he was found dead drunk in the tavern, and was expelled from the church. It was the elder, however, who should have been expelled, because his conduct had been a stumbling-block to a weaker soul.

5. We should be *consistent* in our practice (Rom. 14:14-17). "Let not then your good be evil spoken of" (vs. 16). Our background and associations may give to some wholly innocent matters an ingredient of evil that would make our doing them inconsistent with our Christian testimony and conscience. More than once I heard the late Gypsy Smith relate the story of his father's conversion. He heard the message of salvation, and with penitence received the Saviour as his own. That evening he returned to his motherless children in the gypsy wagon, and related to them all he knew of the Saviour and of the Scriptures. Then he prayed with them, setting up a family altar the first night of his new life in Christ. The following morning he repeated the whole matter again. Then he went back to town, and took with him the dearest treasure of a gypsy's heart, his violin. On returning home that night he was without it, for he had sold it. He had sufficient spiritual insight, the first day of salvation, to realize that the old association of drinking and dancing places, where he had used his violin,

would be inconsistent with his stand for Christ, and detrimental to his own conscience. We are glad for those whose background allows them to play the violin for God's glory; but whatever is inconsistent to us and to others must be abandoned.

6. Is our conduct *constructive?* (Rom. 14:18-19). "Let us therefore . . . follow after the things which make for peace, and things wherewith one may edify another" (vs. 19). There is justifiable and timely irony in the parallel passage, "Now as touching things offered unto idols, we know that we all have knowledge. Knowledge puffeth up, but love edifieth" (I Cor. 8:1). The emphasis is on the word "knowledge," referring to what we allow for ourselves in Christian conduct. This "knowledge," however, is often self-centered into standards of its own, and is utterly oblivious of the feelings or fears of others. Such "knowledge," cocksure and cantankerous, swells us into pride, to the point of our being contemptuous of others, for we can do this or that with a clear conscience; whereas, true Christian love and compassion for our fellow believer would build him up in the faith. In our conduct we have a very real choice at this place. Do my words, actions, standards, make for peace, to establish others in the truth of the gospel; or do I live to myself, unconcerned about the blessing promised to the peacemakers (Matt. 5:9) or about building strong Christian character and convictions in those that are as yet weaker in the faith? In that same vein is the admonition to consideration for others, "Brethren, if a man

be overtaken in a fault, ye which are spiritual, restore such an one in the spirit of meekness; considering thyself, lest thou also be tempted. Bear ye one another's burdens, and so fulfil the law of Christ" (Gal. 6:1,2).

7. We should be careful of *conscience* in what we allow in Christian conduct (Rom. 14:20-23). "Happy is he that condemneth not himself in that thing which he alloweth" (vs. 22). Careful, I repeat, of conscience, our own as well as that of others. "Hast thou faith?" (vs. 22), does not refer to saving faith in Christ, rather to faith or confidence that our conduct is correct according to the standards of God's Word. If so, happy are we under the blessing of the Lord; but there is condemnation of conscience if we act without that confidence. "Whatsoever is not of faith (confidence in our conduct) is sin" (vs. 23). The admonition can be stated in elementary terms: if it is doubtful, it is wrong for you. One remembers the account of the Scotsman who had a dress shirt, to be worn on special occasions. After he had used it several times he would question the cleanliness of the linen, and possibly take it to the window for better light. His wife's words were very wise, "If it's doubtful, it's dirty."

We have to live with our own conscience, to be under self-condemnation as well as under the conviction of the Spirit when our deeds are doubtful to ourselves; and on the other hand, we can have the happiness of a good conscience. We are to bear in mind also, however, the conscience of others in that which we allow. "But take heed lest by any means this liberty of yours become a stumbling-block to them that are weak. For if any man see thee which hast knowledge sit at meat in the idol's temple, shall not the conscience of him which is weak be emboldened to eat those things which are offered to idols; and through thy knowledge shall the weak brother perish, for whom Christ died? But when ye sin so against the brethren, and wound their weak conscience, ye sin against Christ" (I Cor. 8:9-12). Strong and searching words, that should give us a tender and thoughtful conscience, with conviction that "Wherefore, if meat make my brother to offend (stumble), I will eat no flesh while the world standeth, lest I make my brother to offend" (vs. 13). High standard? Yes, high, but also holy and helpful; with the conscience of a weaker Christian as my criterion.

8. The final criterion is the capstone of them all: is our conduct *Christ-like?* (Rom. 15:1-7). "Let every one of us please his neighbor for his good to edification. For even Christ pleased not himself. . . ." (vss. 2, 3). Is the welfare and well-being of others a first consideration with us, as it was with Him? Can we deny ourselves, that we might please others (vs. 1)? Is any sacrifice on our part in the least commensurate with His sacrifice for us? He has been patient with us, and desires that we be "like-minded one toward another according to Christ Jesus" (vs. 5). Do our words and our deeds, our attitudes and our acts, show

forth Christ to others, especially to the weak in the faith? Are we Christlike in our consideration and concern for them?

Non-conformity to the world, non-condemnation of others, convictions, consideration, consistency, constructiveness, conscience, and a Christlike attitude; these are criteria of Christian conduct, the spirit and not the letter of divine law! Let us apply them to our action, in the light of another's conscience. Liquor and tobacco are clearly out of keeping with these standards. The movies—the good ones, you say? The question is—are there "good ones," or is there the mixture of passion and depravity with all for box office receipts? Does the clean come out of the unclean? Roger Babson wonders why sensible Americans contribute so much to education and civic welfare, and allow all to be undermined by an hour in the movies at night. Would not my attendance at "good movies" prove a stumbling-block to weaker Christians, whose standards of conduct might be less informed than mine? Are the movies worldly, or Christlike? Is not a high standard of separation worthwhile, for the welfare of others; for if movies make my brother to stumble, I will not attend as long as the world stands.

We have the same problem in the radio programs we hear or in the magazines we read. After a season of deep spiritual awakening at Wheaton College one freshman girl settled the radio problem by posting on her radio, "This radio is dedicated to the Lord Jesus

Christ." The places we attend are before us; and it seems to me that baseball and football would be put in the clear, but prize-fighting would not be. A stick of wood and a ball—fine, as long as you *hit* the ball, as in baseball or golf, but do not push it around as in pool. Why? because of the association of the latter with pool halls. Our dress should be conservative and in good taste. Our Lord would not have us to be startling and "smart," nor to be scarecrows. The Lord's Day is especially important, in my opinion; for it is dedicated unto His service. The world watches the Christian, to see if he will conform to its standards of utter disregard for the sanctity of the day. Happy is that Christian who condemns not himself nor causes others to stumble by the places he attends, purchases he makes, paper he reads, programs he hears, on the Lord's Day.

This is the discipline of desire, that we measure what we want to do by criteria of Christian conduct, with desire to be Christlike and Christ honoring in all we do, that others may see Him in us.

Our desires must be disciplined by obedience to Christ, lest they be destructive of the faith of others, not to speak of ourselves. We cannot please ourselves and please the Lord Jesus as well. To follow our own inclinations is to be indifferent to the spiritual welfare of others, especially of those who are new and weak in the faith. To say that there is no Scripture against one's "Christian liberty" is to repeat in substance the sneer of Cain: "Am I my brother's keeper?" Undisciplined desire can undo the standards of that one who looks to an older and more experienced Christian for the example and encouragement that are badly needed. It can prove to be a stone of stumbling rather than the building stone that he requires.

By way of contrast, the desire that is disciplined to seek the welfare of others and to deny one's self, to consider responsibility rather than liberty, to be charitable, constant, consistent, constructive and Christ-like, such desire will strengthen the wavering Christian and silence the caustic criticism of the skeptic. The loss of "liberty" involved in the discipline of desire is more than compensated by the spiritual power that it brings into the life. Such discipline is sweetness to ourselves and strength to others.

Past, Present and Future

He was better to me than all my hopes,
    He was better than all my fears;
He made a bridge of my broken works,
    And a rainbow of my tears,
The billows that guarded my sea-girt path
    But carried my Lord on their crest;
When I dwell on the days of my wilderness march
    I can lean on His love for the rest.

He emptied my hands of my treasured store,
    And His covenant love revealed,
There was not a wound in my aching heart,
    But the balm of His breath had healed.
Oh! tender and true was the chastening sore.
    In wisdom, that taught and tried,
Till the soul that He sought was trusting in Him,
    And nothing on earth beside.

THE DISCIPLINE OF
DESOLATION

*"I am withered like grass. But thou, O Lord, shalt
endure forever"* (*Ps.* 102:11, 12).

THE HEART can be so disillusioned
and desolate that it is inarticulate. There were
moments in the life of David, the sweet singer of
Israel, when he could say of himself, "I was dumb
with silence, I held my peace, even from good; and
my sorrow was stirred. . . . But I, as a deaf man, heard
not; and I was as a dumb man that openeth not his
mouth" (Ps. 39:2; 38:13). At other hours of desolation
and distress the heart can describe itself, sometimes
in the depth and beauty of meter tuned to a minor
strain. It was under such circumstances that David
composed Psalm 102 by inspiration of God's Spirit.

Hear his heartfelt and humble complaint, with many
comparisons to portray his feelings: "My days are
consumed like smoke, and my bones are burned as an
hearth. My heart is smitten, and withered like
grass . . . I am like a pelican of the wilderness: I
am like an owl of the desert. I . . . am as a sparrow
alone upon the housetop. . . . My days are like a
shadow that declineth; and I am withered like grass"

(vss. 3-7, 11). Like smoke, grass, pelican, owl, sparrow alone: how desolate can become the human soul!

"My days are consumed like smoke"! How lightly and idly does the smoke drift from the chimney or camp fire. Purposeless and passionless it floats away, to be dissolved into thin air, and leaving behind burnt embers and bitter ashes. Thus can our days be consumed when the heart is desolate; passing without purpose, drifting without direction, fading without feeling for us, leaving only burnt hopes and bitter heartaches. Consumed like smoke!

"My bones are burned as an hearth"! A hearth is the symbol of hospitality and hope, with blaze that beckons and heat that heartens, with warmth that welcomes and grate that gladdens. But when the hearth is cold and cheerless, with no friendly flame within nor flaming friend alongside, how deep the desolation. Burned into the blackness of despair; ashes gray with anguish, cruelly cold with fire unkindled, worthless without warmth of home or hearty friendship. Thus is the heart of the desolate. Burned as an hearth!

"My heart is smitten and withered like grass"! There was a day when the grass was green and new, a delight to man and to beast. How pleasant to the eye of man, how refreshing and restful to his spirit, is the green grass. What a reminder it can be to him of God's goodness and mercy, as the poet sang,

> "This glad green earth, this blue above
> May tell the wonders of Thy love."

In its spring-time beauty and freshness the grass is like the young heart: green, good, glad and a joy to others and to itself. But the grass can become scorched and sere, under summer sun and desolating drought; until it is a symbol of sadness rather than of gladness, of blasted dreams rather than of dreamy blessing, of days that are past forever rather than of promise that is future. Thus is the desolate heart: sere even unto seeming insensibility, yellow even unto seeming uselessness, laid low in languor and listlessness, dry and no longer a delight to any. Withered like grass!

"I am like a pelican of the wilderness"! What a picture of dreariness and desolation: a wilderness, wide and waste, a land of weariness and woe, without habitation or inhabitant except for a lone pelican. His very appearance is pathetic, to say nothing of his best posture and lowly position. No companions, no resting place, no song, no pleasures nor prospects, only solitude and silence. Thus can be the desolate heart: like a pelican in the wilderness!

"I am like an owl of the desert"! The wilderness is weariness enough, and a wasteland; but the desert is utter desolation. Shifting sand under pitiless sun, great rocks and deep gorges, dry watercourses that disfigure the landscape rather than make it a delight, far horizons that hold no prospect for better days except the cruelly maddening mirage that beckons, then bewilders into blinding tears when it turns into nothingness, that is the desert. No lilt of laughter from little children nor light of lover's eye, no friendly fireside nor faithful friends and family, no sight that gladdens nor song that strengthens; only an owl, distant, drab, dreary, doleful. Thus is the desolate heart, like an owl of the desert!

"As a sparrow alone upon the housetop"! The house is symbolical of home and hospitality, hearth and warm hearts, love and laughter, shelter and security; but not the housetop. It faces the unfriendly elements, the extreme heat of summer and bitter cold of winter, the driving rain and the drifting snow, the lightning's flash and the cold starlight, the thunder's roll and the wind's moan. The housetop is outside the house, and is no habitation for the helpless soul, not even for the homeless sparrow. Thus is the desolate heart, outside the habitation of the happy, exposed to pitiless circumstances that sadden the soul already sorrowful and solitary. As a sparrow alone on the housetop!

"Like a shadow that declineth"! The sunshine can be cheery and challenging; but the shadow, cheerless, chill, changeful, chastening. To be sure, the shadow can symbolize the shelter that strengthens, as sang Solomon, "I sat down under his shadow with great delight, and his fruit was sweet to my taste" (Song of Solomon 2:3); but it frequently is the figure of the fearsome and fearful, as David's word, "The valley of the shadow of death" (Ps. 23:4). Steadily although almost imperceptibly, sternly and without hindrance or delay, the shadow lengthens and deepens across life's pathway, and leaves us apprehensive, even anxious about the tomorrows, if there be any. Thus are the days of the desolate heart: drab, dreary, darkening, despairing, like a shadow that declineth!

The desolation of the heart: its silence like the drifting smoke, its bitterness like a burnt hearth, its woeful position like that of a pelican in the wilderness, its doleful outcry like that of a desert owl, its hopeless solitude like that of a sparrow on the housetop, its dreaded sorrow like a shadow that declines; all is summarized in the repeated description of despair, "I am withered as grass" (vs.11). Burned by pitiless sun, blasted by persistent drought, withered into a weary wasteland of utter futility and frustration, without future of usefulness to God or man. Thus is the heart, withered like grass!

"But thou, O Lord, shalt endure forever!" What a difference is brought into life by the little conjunction "but." The whole course of life can be altered by it. The awakened sinner sees his own autobiography in Paul's description of the natural heart of man, and recognizes that all are "by nature the children of wrath, even as others"; and then he reads on, "*but* God, who is rich in mercy, for his great love wherewith he loved us" (Eph. 2:3, 4). We the children of wrath, *but* God rich in mercy who provides salvation from the penalty of sin! Of the Lord Jesus Christ Paul declared at Antioch, "They took him down from the tree, and laid him in a sepulchre. *But* God raised him from the dead" (Acts 13:29, 30). About David it was written, "And Saul sought him every day, *but* God

117

delivered him not into his hand" (I Sam. 23:14). Saul
in his strength and anger, *but* God!

Thus it is with the desolate heart: utterly withered,
but God; and thereby life, with its emptiness and
futility becomes filled with eternal realities. Companions and comforts may be consumed like smoke, but
the Saviour remains, the Compassionate Christ; and in
Him we have more than enough, for time and for
eternity. Heart may be like a hearth, with gray ashes
and dead embers, but He gives "beauty for ashes, the
oil of joy for mourning, the garment of praise for the
spirit of heaviness" (Isa. 61:3). Heart may be
withered as grass, but because of Him, "the wilderness
and the solitary place shall be glad . . . and the desert
shall rejoice, and blossom as the rose" (Isa. 35:1). "He
turneth the wilderness into a standing water, and
dry ground into water-springs. And there he maketh
the hungry to dwell" (Ps. 107:35, 36). Withered like
grass; *but* God!

God will arise, and have mercy upon us (Ps. 102:
13). There comes the moment of His help (vs. 13).
"He will regard the prayer of the destitute, and not
despise their prayer" (vs. 17). He looks from heaven
to see our need (vss. 19-21). Although all else perishes,
He endures; for He is the same, Whose years have no
end (vss. 25-27). All may fail, but God, never!

But God! But God! What strength there is for those
whose days are as smoke; what blessing to those whose
bones are burned as an hearth; what wisdom to those
whose heart is withered like grass; what perseverance

to those who are as pelicans in the wilderness; what delight to those who otherwise are dismal as desert owls; what shelter to those who sit as sparrows alone on the housetop; what assurance to those whose days decline as a shadow; all because He, the Strong One, remains.

This is the discipline of desolation: to see one's days as declining shadows, one's strength as smoke, one's hopes as a burned hearth, one's prospects as a pelican in the pitiless wilderness, one's social needs as a sparrow alone; and to believe, "But thou, O Lord, shalt endure forever!" To fail in this discipline is to be utterly disconsolate and destitute; to find its *truth* is to have our daily delight and defense in Him Who suffers not His faithfulness to fail.

> They took them all away—my toys—
>   Not one was left;
> They set me here, shorn, stripped of
>   humblest joys,
>   Anguished, bereft.

> I wondered why. The years have flown.
>   Unto my hand
> Cling weaker, sadder ones who walk alone—
>   I understand.

In Temptation

Jesus, lover of my soul,
  Let me to Thy bosom fly,
While the nearer waters roll,
  While the tempest still is high!
Hide me, O my Saviour, hide,
  Till the storm of life is past,
Safe into the haven guide,
  O receive my soul at last!

Other refuge have I none;
  Hangs my helpless soul on Thee;
Leave, ah! leave me not alone,
  Still support and comfort me!
All my trust on Thee is stay'd,
  All my help from Thee I bring:
Cover my defenseless head
  With the shadow of Thy wing!

Wilt Thou not regard my call?
  Wilt Thou not accept by prayer?
Lo! I sink, I faint, I fall!
  Lo! on Thee I cast my care!
Reach me out Thy gracious hand!
  While I of Thy strength receive,
Hoping against hope I stand,
  Dying, and behold I live!

—Charles Wesley.

THE DISCIPLINE OF
DESPERATION

"Lord, save me!" (*Matt.* 14:30).

In the Christian life there are hours of distresses, discouragement, darkness, and danger. There are also moments of despair, intense, exacting, excruciating; moments when life and death are in the balance, and we have no strength nor wisdom to top the balance in our favor. We cannot strive nor struggle, flee nor even faint; we can only cry unto God. If He hears us not, and helps us not instantaneously, all is lost. Helpless is the heart that in that brief instant knows not to whom it can cry; on the contrary, happy is the heart, however harrowing may be the experience, that knows Him whose ear is not heavy that He cannot hear nor His arm shortened that He cannot save.

The Scriptures reveal that some of our shortest prayers are our most effectual ones. In artlessness and helplessness Peter cried, "Lord, save me" (Matt. 14:30). We remember the circumstances; and in the split second that is ours to think of his predicament, we might be inclined to believe he had no reasonable cause for his cry. Had he not driven himself into this danger? His had been the shelter of the boat, which, to be sure was in a storm; but it was relatively safe. In his impetuosity, he had said to the shadowy figure on the sea, not visible because of the darkness of the night, "Lord, if it be thou, bid me come unto thee on the water" (vs. 28). Across the waves and through the darkness came in unmistakably sweet and strong tones, "Come" (vs. 29). In immediate and impulsive obedience, he climbed over the side of the boat "to go to Jesus" (vs. 29).

We may not approve his impetuosity nor his human impertinence in attempting to walk on the sea; but we must admire his implicit obedience and his deep devotion to his Lord. Most of us are like the eleven, who did love their Lord, but preferred the security of the ship to the uncertainty of the sea. We will not venture beyond sight and sense, for we are not fools nor fanatics. We adventure little for our Lord; and although we may know the reality of His presence, in darkness and danger, we have never known the strong hand of the Son of Man holding us up from certain and instant disaster, as did Peter. Who can fathom his feelings when, as he began to sink into the dark waves of Galilee where there was no standing, he felt the grasp of that Hand? Only the despairing know what is meant by the words, "And immediately Jesus stretched forth his hand, and caught him, and said unto him, O thou of little faith, wherefore didst thou doubt?" (vs. 31). Doubt, and then a pointed, piercing prayer, "Lord, save me"; and desperation had become the delight of salvation from the sea.

The disciples also had learned something of this discipline of despair that leads to deliverance. They had been with the Lord Jesus on the Sea of Galilee on another night. They had put out to sea at sunset at His express command, "Let us pass over unto the other side" (Mk. 4:35). He was with them in the ship; and exhausted by the labors of the day, He had fallen asleep. "There arose a great storm of wind, and the waves beat into the ship, so that it was being filled" (vs. 37, mg.). The disciples were expert sailors and familiar with the sea, because some had been fishermen thereon; but now their skill and strength were of no avail. Except there be help at once, they were all lost.

In despair they turned to Him still fast asleep on a pillow; and in the urgency of their extremity they cried, "Master, carest thou not that we perish? (vs.38).

That terrible thought, "Carest thou not?" had been forming in their minds as the wind and waves rose higher, and the ship began to founder. Darkness of night, danger of storm, depths of sea with death all about them, then in desperation the disciples gave vent to their pent-up fears, "Carest thou not that we perish?"

The same is true of us today. We are fair-weather followers of the Good Shepherd, and refresh ourselves in green pastures and beside still waters; but as the darkness deepens and the danger rises, we wonder, "Why has He not helped us by now? Does He not care?" The Psalmist knew by firsthand experience the discipline of doubt that precedes that of despair; for he could sing in a minor key, "In the day of my trouble I sought the Lord. . . . I remembered God, and was troubled: I complained, and my spirit was overwhelmed. . . . Will the Lord cast off for ever? . . . **Is his mercy clean gone forever? doth his promise fail for evermore? Hath God forgotten to be gracious? hath he in anger shut up his tender mercies?"** (Ps. 77:2-9).

Our experience can be like his and that of the disciples. For them there was the gracious and immediate response, "And he arose, and rebuked the wind, and said unto the sea, Peace, be still. And the wind ceased, and there was a great calm. . . . And they feared exceedingly, and said one to another, What manner of man is this, that even the wind and the sea obey him?" (Mk. 4:39,41). To be sure, they needed the gentle and searching question, as do we in the moment of despair, "Why are ye so fearful? how is it that ye have no faith?" (vs. 40). For the Psalmist there came the assurance, "Thy way, O God, is in the sanctuary: who is so great a God as our God? Thou art the God that doest wonders: thou hast declared thy strength among the people. . . . Thy way is in the sea, and thy path in the great waters, and thy footsteps are not known" (Ps. 77:13,14,19). The

124

shriek of desperation becomes the song of deliverance!

The unnamed Publican knew this discipline of soul (Luke 18:9-14). He had come to the end of himself. If he had been so minded, like many of his day and ours, he could have blamed his sinful condition upon his family background, his heritage, environment, circumstances, evil companions. He really never had a chance: a poor home, no education, the pitiless strife of the street, ward politics, the dishonesty and trickery of tax-gathering. Of course respectable people like yonder Pharisee despised him; he despised himself. Not only did he not blame his unhappy and unfortunate fate, he also laid no claim to any merit in God's sight, no prayers, no fasting, no tithing, nothing of the Law. He was just a miserable, lost sinner, an "extortioner, unjust" (vs. 11). He could only blame himself, and pray, "God, be merciful to me, a sinner" (vs. 13). And God had mercy upon him, instantly, completely; so that "this man went down to his house justified" (vs. 14).

Discouragement in his struggle against himself and his sin had led him to utter despair: if there be no mercy with God, he was irretrievably lost. His experience was like that of David, who testified, "For day and night thy hand was heavy upon me: my moisture is turned into the drought of summer. I acknowledged my sin unto thee, and mine iniquity have I not hid. I said, I will confess my transgressions unto the Lord; and thou forgavest the iniquity of my sin" (Ps. 32:4,5). The penitent soul that has come to see himself a lost sinner, with no blame on others or claim for merit can also testify. "Out of the depths have I cried unto thee, O Lord. Lord, hear my voice: let thine ears be attentive to the voice of my supplications. If thou, Lord, shouldest mark iniquities, O Lord, who shall stand? But there is forgiveness with thee, that thou mayest be feared" (Ps. 130:1-4). Out of the mire of desperation to the mercy divine, so that there is the song of deliverance from sin!

In his *Thoughts for Life's Journey* the late George Matheson of Scotland re-echoes this discipline of despair. "My soul, reject not the place of thy prostration! It has ever been the robing room for royalty. Ask the great ones of the past what has been the spot of their prosperity; they will say, 'It was the cold ground on which I once was lying.' Ask Abraham; he will point you to the sacrifice of Moriah. Ask Joseph; he will direct you to his dungeon. Ask Moses; he will date his fortune from his danger in the Nile. Ask Ruth; she will bid you build her monument in the field of her toil. Ask David; he will tell you that his songs came from the night. Ask Job; he will remind you that God answered him out of the whirlwind. Ask Peter; he will extol his submission in the sea. Ask John; he will give the palm to Patmos. Ask Paul; he will attribute his inspiration to the light that struck him blind. Ask one more — the Son of Man. Ask Him whence has come His rule over the world. He will answer, 'From the cold ground on which I was lying — the Gethsemane ground; I received my sceptre there.' Thou too, my soul, shalt be garlanded by Gethsemane. The cup thou fain wouldst pass from thee will be thy coronet in the sweet by-and-by. The hour of thy loneliness will crown thee. The day of thy depression will regale thee. It is thy *desert* that will break forth into singing; it is the trees of thy silent *forest* that will clasp their hands."[1]

Danger, darkness, defeat and death before us; and the cry of despair unto the Almighty that brings the crown of deliverance, into safety and light, victory and life! Disciplined by desperation we come to know the Strong Deliverer!

---

[1] George Matheson, *Thoughts for Life's Journeys,* (London: James Claike & Co., 1907), pp. 266, 267.

One By One

One by one the sands are flowing,
  One by one the moments fall;
Some are coming, some are going;
  Do not strive to grasp them all.

One by one thy duties wait thee,
  Let thy whole strength go to each,
Let no future dreams elate thee,
  Learn thou first what these can teach.

One by one (bright gifts from Heaven)
  Joys are sent thee here below;
Take them readily when given,
  Ready too to let them go.

One by one thy griefs shall meet thee,
  Do not fear an armed band;
One will fade as others greet thee;
  Shadows passing through the land.

.   .   .   .

Do not linger with regretting,
  Or for passing hours despond;
Nor, the daily toil forgetting,
  Look too eagerly beyond.

Hours are golden links, God's token,
  Reaching Heaven; but one by one
Take them, lest the chain be broken
  Ere the pilgrimage be done.

—Adelaide A. Procter.*

*From POEMS by Adelaide A. Procter. Used by permission of the publishers, Nimmo, Hay & Mitchell, Edinburgh.

THE DISCIPLINE OF
DETAIL

"For to me to live is Christ" (*Phil.* 1:21).

LIFE HAS ITS occasional crisis that crashes into its commonplaces, but it is more largely made up of details that seem in themselves to be insignificant and unimportant. In the multitude of many duties we may fail altogether to see any pattern to the details of life, and thereby we may miss much of its meaning, not to mention its melody. Details can give the motif, as well as the music, to any life.

Without any stretch of the imagination, life can be likened unto a sentence, in English, or in any other language. A sentence, we recall, is "a combination of words which is complete or expressing a thought, and in writing is usually marked at the close by a period; a sense unit comprising a subject and a predicate, especially one with both subject and finite verb expressed." Incidentally, that sentence is complicated and perhaps difficult to comprehend at first sight. How much like life it is!

Life, like a sentence, should have its subject, expressed or implied. To have self as the subject of one's life sentence is to have narrow horizons, shallow objectives, unsatisfactory achievements; in brief, a life that is wasted. "Whosoever will save his life shall lose it" (Mark 8:35), in this existence, not to speak of eternity. The life with Christ as its grand subject is the life with wide horizons, worthy aims and entirely satisfactory accomplishment. It is the life defined by the Apostle Paul, "For to me to live is Christ" (Phil. 1:21). The measure in which we lose our life for Jesus' sake is the measure of life's breadth, height, depth, motivation and meaning.

The details of a sentence have their significance in life. The Most High puts punctuation marks into our lives, to make them comprehensible and complete. At the moment we may not understand the import of the punctuation, but when the sentence is complete, or even before, we can begin to catch its meaning. A comma indicates a slight change in the direction of the sentence, and an addition to its meaning or enlargement and enrichment to its description. In our impetuosity we want to rush onward toward the conclusion of a given matter; and the Lord begins to add to our lives and to set off that which is new, deeper, and richer by His comma. Let us not be impatient with His apparent change of thought or meaning; rather let us trust that His comma comprehends His compassion and concern for us.

The semicolon indicates a more abrupt and basic change in the direction of the sentence. Quite possibly you have come to a point in life when suddenly the meaning is left unfinished, the light goes out in the sky, the song has turned into silence, or even into a sob; there seems to be neither rhyme nor reason, neither present nor future to your life. The Lord is changing the direction of your life, not to close it, nor to constrain its significance within narrow horizons; on the contrary, He wants to make it broader, deeper, richer; and therefore He puts a semicolon after a given line of thought that you would have desired to have continued.

I have found it so rather frequently in my life. We have enjoyed friends, service, and the like, only to find that the Lord brings to a conclusion such delight that He might use us elsewhere in His service. We were happy and busy on the mission field in Ecuador, and planned to spend all our days in God's glad service there. Young people and older had come to the knowledge of Christ and were preparing themselves to be witnesses among their countrymen. We could visualize no place more useful nor happy. But one day the Lord wrote a semicolon. To be sure, there is then the temptation to feel that life is without meaning, or that the Most High is mistaken in His measures toward us, or that we have failed to heed His guidance. We must remember that circumstances are no criterion of the center of the will of God. Paul and Silas were utterly persuaded of God's call to Macedonia out of a vision of a man therefrom calling to them; and the injustice of their imprisonment in Philippi with its pain and pitiless darkness constituted no evidence that they had been led astray by their own thought or desire. God's semicolon in your life means that He wants to change rather radically the course thereof, that He desires to enlarge its content, and not at all that He has cut you off from or forgotten to be gracious. Some hearts have sat down to sob inconsolably at God's semicolon, and never have gone forward into the clarifying clause that lies beyond. He will make it plain!

Parentheses are indicative of even deeper perplexity than that caused by the semicolon. The whole forward movement of the sentence is suspended and something that seems totally irrelevant is inserted therein. It seems that our lives could do without the interruption, the delay, difficulty, or darkness that has entered. It all seems so entirely without explanation or purpose. We seek to fathom the reason for the sick room and its silence when we sought to serve the Saviour, to decipher the delay and disappointment, to understand the misunderstanding with its tears and apparent tragedy. The parentheses seem inopportune or unimportant, or even impertinent; but there they are.

John Bunyan had reason to be bewildered by life's parentheses. Out of deep darkness and despair he had come to sweet knowledge of salvation through Christ, and had gone forth into His glad service. He had been happy and successful in that service; and then came the long and silent years in Bedford jail. Within that parenthesis he found meaning in God's perplexing providences; and we have learned long afterward more of that apparently pointless period in his life. Let us listen to him:

"I never had in all my life so great an inlet into the Word of God as now . . . Jesus Christ also was never more real and apparent than now — here I have seen and felt Him indeed. . . . I have had sweet sights of the forgiveness of my sins in this place, and of my being with Jesus in another world . . . I never knew what it was for God to stand by me at all times. . . . I had also this consideration, that if I should venture all for God, I engaged God to take care of my concerns. . . . Now was my heart full of comfort. . . . I would not have been without this trial for much: I am comforted every time I think of it, and hope I shall bless God forever for the teachings I have had by it."[1] All of that and more in a parenthesis!

Then there is the period that brings the sentence to its completion. Of course the sentence can conclude with a question mark, if life is essentially an interrogation rather than a statement of fact. If our life reads "For to me to live is Christ," it has a meaning different from the plain statement of the case. Life may be an enigma to us, but we should not be questionable to others. Also, the sentence may end in an exclamation point, with its surprise and astonishment, but hardly with its success. Life should not be an incomplete sentence, whose incompleteness and

---

[1] John Bunyan, *Grace Abounding to the Greatest of Sinners*, chap. 11.

disobedience will not escape the Master. We are to be disciplined by details, to write steadily onward until the sentence stands completed, even to the period.

There are as many kinds of sentences as there are lives. The sentence may be *simple*, not necessarily short, but without complication; it may be *compound*, with two or more independent clauses; it may be *complex*, with modifications qualifying the main clause; it may be *loose*, complex and yet with its meaning appearing early; it may be *periodic*, also complex, but with its meaning not apparent until the last word or almost the last word has been reached; or it may be *balanced*, characterized by symmetry and evenness of flow. Whatever may be the structure of the life, however short or long it may be, wherever it may meander or keep to the beaten track, however many modifications may be made, however confusing it may seem for the time being, it should be meaningful and complete when the conclusion is reached at the period.

Comma, semicolon or colon, parentheses, modifiers, clauses independent and dependent, every detail of the sentence is designed for some purpose. We may be confused when God puts a comma in our life, or sigh inconsolably at a semicolon; we may be utterly perplexed by the apparent irrelevancy of the parenthetical portions which seem to have no connection with the past nor place in the future; we may be muddled by modifiers and be in consternation over some clause; but if our life is His handwriting, if for us "to live is Christ," then every detail can be a delight. The Lord of Life is the Schoolmaster of our life, to make its meaning clear.

> Upon Thy Word I rest
>   Each pilgrim day;
> This golden staff is best
>   For all the way.
> What Jesus Christ hath spoken
> Cannot be broken!
>
> Upon Thy Word I rest,
>   So strong, so sure!
> So full of comfort blest.
>   So sweet, so pure!
> The charter of salvation,
> Faith's broad foundation.
>
> Upon Thy Word I stand,
>   That cannot die;
> Christ seals it in my hand,
>   He cannot lie!
> Thy Word that faileth never,
> Abideth ever.

—Frances Ridley Havergal.

I Love A Tree

I love a tree,
A brave, upstanding tree!
When I am wearied in the strife,
Beaten by storms and bruised by life,
I look up at a tree, and it refreshes me.
If it can keep its head held high,
And look the storms straight in the eye,
Ready to stand, ready to die,
Then by the grace of God can I—
At least with Heaven's help, I'll try;
I love a tree, for it refreshes me!

I love a tree!
When it seems dead,
Its leaves all shorn and bared its head,
When winter flings its cold and snow,
It stands there undismayed by woe;
It stands there waiting for the spring—
A tree is such a believing thing.
I love a tree,
For it refreshes me!

—Ralph Spaulding Cushman.*

*From HILLTOP VERSES AND PRAYERS by Ralph Spaulding Cushman. Copyright 1945. Used by permission of the publishers, Abingdon-Cokesbury Press.

THE DISCIPLINE OF
DETERMINATION

"And having done all, to stand" (*Eph.* 6:13).

Too soon to quit" has become a watchword at Wheaton College; it is a campus countersign of dogged determination to do one's duty with the utmost devotion. Some years ago I read an article with that title that had been prepared and presented by W. J. Cameron on the Ford Sunday Evening Hour program of January 10, 1937. Since then it has been reread or discussed in chapel, with added illustrations from Scripture, at least once a semester. It has become part of Wheaton's philosophy of life, and Wheaton students look forward to its exposition in chapel as one of the college traditions. Through the courtesy and permission of Mr. Cameron the article is here reprinted.

"Young persons sometimes ask Mr. Ford, 'How can I make my life a success?'—as if anyone could answer that question half as well as the one who asks it. But occasionally Mr. Ford does give a valuable tip, even if at the moment the young person receiving it fails to appreciate it. One such tip would be—

'If you start a thing, finish it.' It sounds rather familiar, a piece of old-fashioned advice—but it is part of an engineer's design for living — finish it!

"'Yes,' one says, 'but the thing may not be worth finishing.' Of course, when he says 'finish it,' Mr. Ford isn't thinking about the thing at all, he is thinking about you—you, Miss Maiden, and you, Sir Youth. In the preparatory time of life the real job is not what you are working on, but what it is doing to you. You start it with a great gush of interest—you miss your meals for it—then suddenly it goes stale—and you quit. Or you find that your plan is wrong—and you quit. And all that you have as profit from your effort is the knowledge of how to quit. 'Well,' you say, 'the thing wasn't worth it!' Quite probably, but you are, and that's the whole point.

"Plausible reasons for quitting are always at hand. Mr. Ford told us one day that when he was making his first car in that little brick building on the alley in the rear of his home, he worked away with all the ardor of young enthusiasm looking forward to great results. Then the thrill and the interest simply evaporated. Why? He said he had gone far enough on that first car to see how he could build a second and a better one, and the glowing new vision got in the way of his work. What was the use of finishing the car he had started? Some untaught inner wisdom must have warned him, for he forced himself on. He soon discovered he was learning more and more about his second car by going on to complete his first. But so strong was the temptation to quit that he realizes now it was precisely that—a temptation to quit, not merely an urge to do better—and had he yielded, he might have failed to finish the second car too. So, here is one plausible reason for dropping a thing unfinished—the chance to start something better.

"Another handy reason for quitting is just the opposite—we want to quit, not because we think we see something better, but because we see nothing at all;—so, why continue? Why not throw up the sponge? Well, that depends. Was this thing laid on you to do? Were your motives sound? Had you a clear right and a clear reason to start it? Very well—what has happened? Oh, a cloud has settled down and you cannot see? Well, many a man has never seen the light he needed, or the work he needed, until he entered that cloud and walked through it. Following faithfully on never leads anyone into permanent darkness. But for the quitter, all he is likely to get is a stronger habit of quitting and a lower place to begin again. The man who will not give up, even if he fail of his objective, is led through to another objective; the man who hangs on as if he were paid to hang on can always start again at par or better—he has strengthened himself.

"Most of us are where we are for a very good reason. This is our post which has no one to hold it but us. If we abandon it, we discover that it is something in ourselves we abandon. Just keeping on, through the most hopeless aspect of keeping on, may be the important act of one's career. The last dejected effort often becomes the winning stroke! After years of observation one is ready to say that most of the people one has seen quit have quit too soon. Another week; a few more good licks; standing by just a little longer—and the whole situation would have opened into a larger phase. But, no! they were more practiced in quitting than in staying. Only recently one saw a man quit in spite of earnest counsel because he couldn't get what he wanted; two days later the very thing he wanted came looking for him, and he wasn't there. He had quit too soon. It is always too soon to quit.

"The theater of this drama is ourselves; the mind may forge a circumstance into a shackle, or it may lift us into the sphere where events are plastic. The power of courage and endurance to rearrange our whole relation to events is proved daily as one of our commonest experiences. In its lowliest form, this compulsion, this power, is simply the act of hanging on, plodding on, doggedly forcing oneself on for yet one hour or one more day. Persisted in, against all odds and all reasons, this attitude leads through—it does lead through. Quitting makes a dead end of any road —often just as it was ready to open. Transfer if you must; catch another wave-length; change your level to a higher one, but don't quit—it is always too soon to quit."

Determination to finish what we have begun is a discipline we need. We trifle with one task, and when it becomes trite we want a change of scenery. Every semester several come to me to bid farewell, with work unfinished. Were they led of God to Wheaton? Has some other place, or person, or project become more pleasing than the routine of studies? They think that just over the horizon there are greater advantages and opportunities. Some glowing vision dazzles them, and they cannot stick to their appointed duty.

Pre-eminently is this discipline exemplified in the life of our Lord Jesus Christ. At an early age He was about His Father's business (Luke 2:49). In the strength of manhood He declared, "My meat is to do the will of him that sent me, and finish his work" (John 4:34). When earthly service was complete He could pray, "I have finished the work which thou gavest me to do" (John 17:4); and from Calvary's Cross rang out His triumph, "It is finished" (John 19:30).

Can we not follow His footsteps, filled with His Spirit, to finish the task appointed, with heart aglow and hurrying feet, with strong hands and steady mind, with shield of faith and sword of the Spirit, with patience to run the race that is set before us? Can we not trust Him for grace that is sufficient, for strength that is perfected in weakness, for help that is sure, and for faithfulness that will not fail, in order that we may know the discipline of doing our duty? Then it is always too soon to quit.

On His Blindness

When I consider how my light is spent
  Ere half my days in this dark world and wide,
  And that one Talent which is death to hide
  Lodged with me useless, though my soul more bent
To serve therewith my Maker, and present
  My true account, lest He returning chide;
  "Doth God exact day-labor, light denied?"
I fondly ask. But Patience, to prevent
That murmur, soon replies, "God doth not need
  Either man's work or his own gifts. Who best
  Bear his mild yoke, they serve him best. His state
Is kingly: thousands at his bidding speed,
  And post o'er land and ocean without rest;
  They also serve who only stand and wait."

—John Milton.

THE DISCIPLINE OF
DIFFICULTY

"And he arose, and followed him" (*Matt.* 9:9).

ONE OFTEN stands silent upon see-
ing the difficulties some sanguine souls must surmount
in order to do their lifework. *The Conquest of Peru,*
with its companion *The Conquest of Mexico,* is known
by all to stand securely among the immortal pieces
of historical writing; but not many seem to be aware
of the immense physical handicaps under which it
was composed. Its author, William H. Prescott,[1] in
unassuming manner told his own story in the pre-
face of his epochal account of Atahuallpa, Pizarro,
Almagro, and others.

"While at the University, I received an injury in
one of my eyes, which deprived me of sight of it.
The other, soon after, was attacked by inflammation so severely, that, for some time, I lost the sight
of that also, and though it was subsequently restored,
the organ was so much disordered as to remain per-
manently debilitated, while twice in my life since,

---

[1] William H. Prescott, *History of the Conquest of Peru,* (Philadelphia:
J. B. Lippincott & Co., 1874) Vol. I, pp. 16-20.

I have been deprived of the use of it for all purposes of reading and writing, for several years together. It was during one of these periods that I received from Madrid the materials for the 'History of Ferdinand and Isabella,' and in my disabled condition, with my Transatlantic treasures lying around me, I was like one pining from hunger in the midst of abundance. In this state, I resolved to make the ear, if possible, do the work of the eye. I procured the services of a secretary, who read to me the various authorities; and in time I became so far familiar with the sounds of the different foreign languages (to some of which indeed, I had been previously accustomed by a residence abroad), that I could comprehend his reading without much difficulty. . . .

"Still another difficulty occurred, in the mechanical labor of writing, which I found a severe trial to the eye. This was remedied by means of a writing-case, such as is used by the blind, which enabled me to commit my thoughts to paper without the aid of sight, serving me equally well in the dark as in the light. . . .

"Though I was encouraged by the sensible progress of my work, it was necessarily slow. But in time the tendency to inflammation diminished, and the strength of the eye was confirmed more and more. It was at length so far restored, that I could read for several hours of the day, though my labors in this way necessarily terminated with the daylight. . . .

"But a change has again taken place during the

last two years. The sight of my eye has become gradually dimmed, while the sensibility of the nerve has been so far increased, that for several weeks of the last year I have not opened a volume, and through the whole time I have not had the use of it, on a average, for more than an hour a day. . . .

"From this statement—too long, I fear, for his patience—the reader, who feels any curiosity about the matter, will understand the real extent of my embarrassments in my historical pursuits. That they have not been very light will be readily admitted, when it is considered that I have had but a limited use of my eye, in its best state, and that much of the time I have been debarred from the use of it altogether. Yet the difficulties I have had to contend with are very far inferior to those which fall to the lot of a blind man. I know of no historian, now alive, who can claim the glory of having overcome such obstacles, but the author of 'La Conquete de l'Angleterre par les Normands'; who, to use his own touching and beautiful language, 'has made himself the friend of darkness'; and who, to a profound philosophy that requires no light but that from within, unites a capacity for extensive and various research, that might well demand the severest application of the student."

This is the discipline of difficulty, understood and overcome only by the indomitable in heart. Only the undaunted, despite aching head and failing sight, could say that others could be in deeper difficulty than they. Lesser souls would be swallowed up in their own sickness, sorrows and silence.

John Milton knew the deeper discipline of total blindness. Gifted, brilliant, with educational advantages beyond many of his contemporaries, spiritually-minded, he became blind at the age of forty-four, when his countrymen were in the throes of controversy between King and Commonwealth. Milton's public service continued for some time; but blindness became in time an insuperable barrier to such service. Far from bemoaning his cruel fate or becoming embittered by the narrowed horizons of his life, he brought forth his immortal masterpieces, *Paradise Lost, Paradise Regained,* and *Samson Agonistes.* A blind man could see Paradise, and has helped countless others to see it down through the generations since his day! What blind man would not have questioned God's demands of him saying,

"Doth God exact day-labor, light denied? I fondly ask."

With the penetration and patience of a puritan, with unshaken faith in the justice and kindness of the Most High, he concluded:

"They also serve who only stand and wait."

Who wanted a blind man for service higher than that of country? No man, but God did!

All difficulties in life are not physical, although these loom large in our thoughts. Physical handicaps break some men and women; and others are forced thereby to a larger usefulness, as was the case with Milton. Moses, for example had the handicap of age before he began his lifework. At forty, when life allegedly begins, he went into exile, to spend his days as an obscure shepherd of the desert. He endured the adjustments made necessary by the shifting from Pharaoh's majestic court to a Midian sheepfold, with its solitude, silence and apparent uselessness. At eighty, when most men have retired from active service, he was called at the burning bush to become the Deliverer of his people. With reasons, he could object to this calling, saying, "Who am I, that I should go unto Pharaoh, and that I should bring forth the children of Israel out of Egypt?" (Exod. 3:11). Who would want an unknown old man as a leader to organize unruly and untutored tribes into a nation, and to lead them to the land of promise? No man, perhaps, would want him; but God did. He was God's man, despite any human handicap.

Mordecai knew the humanly hopeless handicap of racial prejudice. He was a Jew in a strange land, and knew by experience the bitterness of unbridled racial bigotry. He had to warn his niece, Esther, not to reveal her nationality (Esther 2:20). Haman's wrath knew no bounds when he was told that Mordecai was a Jew (3:4); with the result that he "sought to destroy all the Jews that were throughout the whole kingdom of Ahasuerus, even the people of Mordecai" (3:6). The plot proceeded temporarily without hin-

147

drance, to the pleasure of Haman; while Mordecai was overcome with fear and grief (4:1-3). Only the soul that has felt the heel of the oppressor and the fury of the sadist can sense the sorrow that was Mordecai's.

However, he was not overcome by these apparently insurmountable difficulties. After the sackcloth and ashes there was the arising to trust God for help. Vigorous, even dangerous methods were devised: the Queen was to ask unbidden audience with the King, a move which possibly could have proved fatal to her (4:16). There was to be prayer and fasting, within the palace of the Queen, and without; and "Mordecai went his way, and did according to all that Esther had commanded him" (4:17). Who could help a man rendered helpless and hopeless by blind and bitter prejudice? No man, but God could help him in his difficulty; and He did!

Matthew the publican knew the stinging social prejudice that can be heaped in scorn upon the outcast. The publican was a pestiferous pariah to the Palestinian of our Lord's day. He was an apostate, a renegade, who had sold himself to be the servant of the hated Romans. A customs officer, the cur! A tax gatherer, the grafter! A tool of Imperial Rome, the traitor! No contempt or contumely was adequate for the unspeakable publican. By their logic the people classified the publican with the lowest of the population: the sinners. Therefore they asked the disciples of our Lord in the house of Matthew, as on other similar occasions, "Why eateth your Master with publicans and sinners?" (Matt. 9:11; Luke 15:2; etc.).

However, Matthew was not overcome by social stigma. As he sat at the receipt of customs he had heard words of inexpressible beauty and blessing: "Follow me" (Matt: 9:9). Without hesitation he had arisen to follow the Lord Jesus Christ. No handicap of social status, of family background, of the opinions of others, deterred him. Matthew would follow the Master. The social outcast became the servant of the Saviour and the human author of the gospel narrative that bears his name. Who would have thought that the Prince of life would have had pleasure in the service of an ostracized publican? No man, perhaps; but the Lord Jesus did.

Herein lies the discipline of difficulty: to recognize one's limitations and handicaps; nevertheless, to rise up and do the impossible in spite of them. To yield to discouragement and difficulty is to be defeated. The handicap, I repeat, can be physical, racial, social, personal in any way; yet the soul that will rise up and follow the Saviour will know life that climbs with Bunyan's Pilgrim the Hill Difficulty, to find on its summit the Palace Beautiful, whose windows face the sun-rising. Our discipline is to keep on climbing when sight is dim and strength is debilitated, when friends fail and foes are fierce, when handicaps hinder and hardships harry. God has use for the heart that no difficulties can deter!

Looking Unto God

I look to Thee in every need
    And never look in vain;
I feel thy strong and tender love,
    And all is well again:
The thought of Thee is mightier far
Than sin and pain and sorrow are.

Discouraged in the work of life,
    Disheartened by its load,
Shamed by its failures or its fears,
    I sink beside the road;
But let me only think of Thee,
And then new heart springs up in me.

Thy calmness bends serene above
    My restlessness to still;
Around me flows thy quickening life,
    To nerve my faltering will;
Thy presence fills my solitude;
Thy providence turns all to good.

Embosomed deep in Thy dear love,
    Held in Thy law, I stand;
Thy hand in all things I behold,
    And all things in Thy hand;
Thou leadest me by unsought ways,
And turn'st my mourning into praise.

—Samuel Longfellow

THE DISCIPLINE OF
DISABILITY

"The things which happened unto me" (*Phil.* 1:12).

So MUCH of life seems utterly mean-
ingless, even miserable, without rhyme or reason,
right or wrong, and justice, least of all. There is
abundance everywhere of turmoil and trouble, tragedy
and tears, inhumanity and injustice, sickness and
sorrow, so that anyone without could reason that the
universe is entirely unreasonable, a miserable mess,
a ghastly joke. There is so much that just "happens,"
no apparent plan nor purpose, only pathos, pain, and
perplexity, loneliness instead of love, handicaps instead of help, false hopes instead of far horizons, pain
instead of pleasure, inactivity instead of activity, sobs
instead of song, four walls instead of four freedoms,
darkness instead of daylight, futility instead of fulfillment: these happen to all of us. This is life; but not
all of it.

There is the discipline of disability that brings singing for sighing, serving for sitting, gladness for gloom,
assurance for ashes, melody for mourning, usefulness
for uselessness, duty for dungeons. Some brave souls
have trusted in cruel trials, have sung in dark shadows,

have believed in blinding bewilderment, have waited for divine aid when assailed by diabolical wickedness. They have beyond the testings, tragedies, and tears of time held to the truth of Romans 8:28, "And we know that all things work together for good to them that love God, to them who are the called according to his purpose."

Joseph knew this discipline. Envy by his elder brothers and hatreds within his own home sold him into slavery on foreign soil (Gen. 37). For efficiency and effectiveness in Potiphar's household he was rewarded with misrepresentation and miscarriage of justice, and was bound in prison (Gen. 39). For cooperation in that dismal place and for consideration toward Pharaoh's butler and baker he was forgotten and forsaken (Gen. 40). However, other days came: the opening of prison doors (Gen. 41:14); the service in high places (41:43); the blessing of God to the extent that he could name his first-born Manasseh ("Forgetting"—"for God hath made me forget all my toil, and all my father's house," vs. 51), and the second son Ephraim ("Fruitful"—"For God hath caused me to be fruitful in the land of my affliction," vs. 52); and finally, the bowing down of his own brothers to him (42:6; 43:26; 44:14). To them he could say, "Now therefore be not grieved, nor angry with yourselves, that ye sold me hither: for God did send me before you to preserve life. . . . And God sent me before you to preserve you a posterity in the earth. . . . So now it was not you that sent me hither, but God" (Gen.

45:5,7,8). Not you, your envy, malice or hatred; not you, but God! Later he added, "But as for you, ye thought evil against me: but God meant it unto good" (50:20). Your thought, evil; God's thought, for good. For Joseph, and even unto his brothers, everything worked together for good.

Job knew this discipline. He was happy, wholesome, helpful to others, and holy before God, who described him as "none like him in the earth, a perfect and an upright man" (Job 1:8); yet in a brief time there came loss of loved ones, wealth, and health, everything. To side with his "comforters," cocksure of themselves and sometimes caustic, and say that Job's sorrow was the result of his sin, is to make the story without significance. It is only logical and reasonable that foolishness and folly should have their fruitage in judgment; but in the book of Job God is teaching us an even dozen lessons: there can be sorrow without sin, darkness without disobedience, inequity without iniquity, mourning without merit, chaos without cause, judgment without justice. The innocent suffer because of the folly of the fathers, the greed of the grafters, the arrogance of the autocrats, the laxity of the laws, the inhumanity of the uninhibited, the treachery of the tyrants, the wickedness of war, the fatality of fortune, the godlessness of the ungodly.

Without understanding that not all sorrow is the result of our own sin, that loss of loved ones and health can bring one into "the dark night of the soul," and that God has a way of release for the sorrowing saint with a reward for his sighing, the book of Job would be completely enigmatical and incomprehensible to us. "The dark night of the soul" can bring us into bondage, test our trust in God, cast away our confidence, perplex our perspective, befuddle our faculties, until like Job we bewail the day of our birth (3:1-18), fail to find God (23:8,9), and desire death (17:14-16). To be sure, there are streaks of light shining through the dark clouds: "I know that my redeemer liveth" (19:25), and "He knoweth the way that I take: when he hath tried me, I shall come forth as gold" (23:10); but these are the rare exceptions in Job's dark experience. Job was in the bleak, bitter blackness of the night, to which it seemed there would never come a dawn.

Such severe testing times for the soul are not unknown among God's dear children, when the heart is utterly desolate, the mind dark, hope dim, and help delayed. It seems that no "comforters" can console them at such a time, neither by sound counsel nor strong courage, least of all, by condemnation for alleged sin. "The dark night of the soul" seems to be a valley to be traversed alone, like Christian in the Valley of the Shadow of Death. The pathway is precarious, the enemy accuses, the abyss yawns, the heart fails; but if the darkened soul will go on, the morning will come. It did for Christian in *Pilgrim's Progress;* it did for Job. "And the Lord turned the captivity of Job, when he prayed for his friends: also the Lord gave Job twice as much as he had before. . . . So the Lord blessed the latter end of Job more than his beginning" (42:10,12). Therefore the Scriptures say of him, "Ye have heard of the patience of Job, and have seen the end of the Lord; that the Lord is very pitiful, and of tender mercy" (Jas. 5:11).

The blessing of the Lord! The end of the Lord! The pity and the mercy of the Lord! It all worked together for good to Job; and his testimony has blessed countless millions of believers down the ages.

Jonah knew this discipline. Unlike Job, who came under its rigorous regimen because of no fault of his own, Jonah was exercised thereby because of his disobedience. He knew the will of God for his life, and fled from it. Imagine a human heart that desired to run away "from the presence of the Lord" (Jonah 1:3). Tempest was his lot, within his own soul as well as in the sea, and terror the lot of his companions, until he testified of his failure. Who can appreciate or analyze his feelings as he fell into the raging sea and into the fearsome sepulchre of the great fish? Darkness, utter despair, imminent death were his portion. "Out of the belly of hell" (2:2) he cried unto the Lord in penitence and faith, saying, "I am cast out of thy sight; yet I will look again toward thy holy temple. . . . When my soul fainted within me I remembered the Lord. . . . I will pay that that I have vowed. Salvation is of the Lord" (2:4,7,9). Despairing, fainting, repentant he returned unto the Lord,

Who delivered him from certain death (2:10), and called him the second time (3:1). In contrast with Job's long darkness, the discipline of Jonah was relatively brief, dramatic, and equally effective. It "worked together for good," for he learned, "Salvation is of the Lord" (2:9).

In eminent degree the Apostle Paul knew this discipline. At Damascus' gate he had been clearly called to salvation and service (Acts 9:3-6; 26:12-20). He had served the Lord in many cities and countries, through many dangers on land and sea, at the risk of his life; and had been very successful in that service. One would be inclined to expect that in the latter days of his strenuous life there would be some respite from its rigours; on the contrary, matters seemed to grow worse. There was the tumult in Jerusalem (Acts 21:27—22:24); and these were the successive prisons of Jerusalem (22:24), Caesarea (23:23—26:32), and Rome (28:16).

Obviously, the Christians of his day were perplexed by Paul's long imprisonment, with the slight possibility of his ever again being free. Apparently the believers at Philippi had expressed their anxiety and apprehension, to which he made reply: "But I would ye should understand, brethren, that the things which happened unto me have fallen out rather unto the furtherance of the gospel" (Phil. 1:12). Injustice, intrigue, insolence, imprisonment, all that "happened" had advanced the real purpose of Paul's life!

He had learned that discipline in lesser degree in days gone by. The first plot against his life had showed him the providence of God (Acts 9:22-25); the perversity of the sorcerer had given opportunity for the power of God to be shown (13:6-12); the persecution at Antioch had pointed the Gentiles to the Saviour (13:44-49); the prison of Philippi had provided opportunity to witness to prisoners and jailers (16:25-34). In each case he could affirm the testimony of David, "Many are the afflictions of the righteous: but the Lord delivereth him out of them all" (Ps. 34:19). The imprisonment in Rome provided effective witness to the guard (Phil. 1:13). It has given encouragement to fearful fellow believers, even until our day (1:14). It has shed light on the deepest truth of the gospel: "to me to live is Christ, and to die is gain" (1:21). It provided the opportunity, by the inspiration of God's Holy Spirit, to write the Prison Epistles. Truly, all that "happened" furthered the gospel. It worked together for good!

What "happens" to you and me may not be envy, neglect, loss, darkness, disobedience, despair, narrow horizons; but in the "center of the circle of the will of God" all that happens comes "from His dear hand." God means it for good; He is pitiful and merciful. It works together for good; it furthers His purpose of our life. "Salvation is of the Lord!" we are taught in the discipline of disability.

Fulfillment

"My words . . . which shall be fulfilled in their
season."

"Not one word hath failed of all He hath promised—
all came to pass."

Fulfillment!
Ah, 'tis a lovely word!
After all the weary years,
After all the pain and tears,
After all the doubts and fears,—
Fulfillment!

Fulfillment!
Yes, every promise kept!
After waiting, longing, dread,
After brightest hopes have fled,
Lo, it is done, as He hath said—
Fulfillment!

Fulfillment!
Such as ye cannot contain!
Good measure pressed-down, running o'er,
All He hath shown and so much more,
A rending sky—an open door!
Fulfillment!

—Frances Metcalfe.

THE DISCIPLINE OF

DISAPPOINTMENT

"I had no relief for my spirit" (*II Cor.* 2:13,R.V.).

W<small>HO HAS</small> not experienced the depths of discouragement that come from the stinging defeat of eager expectations, the merciless blasting of high and happy hopes, the frustrations of fond dreams; in a word, from disappointment, dark, deep, dismal?

We had not planned the results in that way. We needed friends and helpers, whose word was true, whose co-operation was cheerful and constructive, and whose dependability was undoubted, but they failed us. We needed abundance of physical health to perform our tasks, and our strength was pitifully poor. We needed large resources to achieve a worthy goal, for the glory of God, and our resources were woefully inadequate. We needed encouragement and enthusiasm, and our only reward was caustic criticism or studied indifference. We believed human promises that proved to be puffs of wind; we experienced pain rather than gain. We were disappointed.

Had we been at fault our anguish of spirit would have been less excruciating, but we trusted others, we tried to conserve our resources, physical and material, we did our very best; only to be disappointed. For our effort and sacrifice we suffer disillusionment, despair and possible defeat. We turn to self-pity, that eats like an acid into the fabric of our hearts, and likewise defiles others. Why go on, why keep on trying, why smile, why trust anybody? With air castles dissolved by disappointment, why not sulk in our tents and seek to heal our wounded spirit by disdain toward others?

Disillusionment, despair, defeat and degrading self-pity do not meet nor mend disappointment. Going onward does. An excellent example is found in the experience of the Apostle Paul as recorded in II Corinthians 2:12-14. He had anticipated meeting Titus at the old city of Troas (Troy), but Titus did not put in appearance. There is no indication in the sacred record as to why he did not come, only that Paul was restless in spirit. How did he react to that disappointment? He kept right on going, thankful for the assurance that the Most High "always leadeth us in triumph in Christ" (vs. 14, A.R.V.).

Thankfulness helps. A thankful spirit remembers the many triumphs as well as the trials of our faith, the many promises in the Word as well as the many perils by the way. Paul was thankful under a wide variety of circumstances: thankful for food and shelter in the midst of a storm that threatened his life (Acts 27:35); thankful for faithful brethren in distant places (Rom. 1:8; I Cor. 1:4; Phil. 1:3; etc.), thankful above all else for the Lord Jesus Christ, God's unspeakable gift (II Cor. 9:15). Therefore, he could urge us to be thankful in all things (Col. 3:15; Eph. 5:20), especially in prayer (Phil. 4:6; Col. 4:2), as we make known our requests. A heart that is thankful to God for His many mercies is conditioned by a sweetness of God's spirit against the bitterness of human disappointment.

God's people have always found it to be so. David knew disappointment and discouragement too deep for further tears, but he "encouraged himself in the Lord his God" (I Sam. 30:6). He could say, "Deep calleth unto deep at the noise of thy waterspouts: all thy waves and thy billows are gone over me. Yet the Lord will command his lovingkindness in the daytime, and in the night his song shall be with me, and my prayer unto the God of my life" (Ps. 42:7,8). Habakkuk saw no outward prospect of prosperity, only utter desolation and disappointment, yet a thankful heart lifted him to high places of victory. "Although the fig tree shall not blossom, neither shall fruit be in the vines; the labour of the olive shall fail, and the fields shall yield no meat; the flock shall be cut off from the fold, and there shall be no herd in the stalls: Yet I will rejoice in the Lord, I will joy in the God of my salvation. The Lord God is my strength, and he will make my feet like hinds' feet, and he will make me to walk upon mine high places" (Hab. 3:17-19). Paul could be thankful to God even though others had failed, and could walk on with Him. Try thankfulness when tempted to despair.

Assurance helps. Paul was certain that, although he had been disappointed, he could be led in triumph in Christ or, as one translation (Moffat) renders that statement: "Wherever I go, thank God, he makes my life a constant pageant of triumph in Christ, diffusing the perfume of His knowledge everywhere by me." Out of wide experience and deep trials, he had been lifted above human considerations, for he had learned that "all things work together for good to them that love God" (Rom. 8:28). He could stand steadfast in his devotion to Christ even if he stood humanly alone, for he could say, "All men forsook me . . . Notwithstanding the Lord stood with me, and strengthened me" (II Tim. 4:16,17). He could endure weakness, infirmities, necessities, distresses, even take pleasure in them, for he had learned that when he was weak in himself, he could be strong in Christ, whose grace was sufficient for him (II Cor. 12:9,10). He could be satisfied with whatever provision his Master made for him, for he had learned in whatever state he found himself, therewith to be content. He could do all things through Christ, who strengthened him (Phil. 4:11-13).

Do we know the assurance of trust that takes the sting out of disappointment and turns it rather to "His appointment"? Joseph could say, "It was not you that sent me hither, but God" (Gen. 45:8). The Most High had so sweetened Joseph's spirit that he named his sons Manasseh ("Forgetting") and Ephraim ("Fruitfulness"), for God made him to forget his disappointment and to be fruitful in the land of affliction (Gen. 41:51,52).

Paul had been disappointed in John Mark, but later learned that "he is profitable to me for the ministry" (II Tim. 4:11). The Lord Jesus was disappointed in Peter, but He prayed for him that he would turn again to be strength to the early Christians (Luke 22:31,32). What would happen if in faith and love we prayed for those who had disappointed us? Would not they turn to the Saviour, would not our hearts be sweetened, and would not life become "a constant pageant of triumph in Christ"? Be assured of God's promise, as was Paul, who could say, "the things which happened unto me have fallen out rather unto the furtherance of the gospel" (Phil. 1:12). Try faith in God and in our fellows when we face disappointment.

Going on helps. Rather than sulk by life's roadside, Paul went to the next place of service. There were many that needed his ministry of love, to whom his life, by the indwelling Saviour, could be the unspeakably sweet fragrance of Christ. Herein lies the real discipline of disappointment and despair, to rise up to help others, and to find in that very attitude and act, that life is "a constant pageant of triumph in Christ." Ezekiel could rise out of the sorrow caused by his wife's sudden death to bring the message of God to his people on the morrow (Ezek. 24:18). Out of bitter disillusionment Hosea could say, "Then shall we know, if we follow on to know the Lord" (Hos. 6:3). Of the Lord Jesus, Isaiah prophesied, "He shall

not fail nor be discouraged" (Isa. 42:4). Tidings came
to Him about the tragic death of His cousin, John the
Baptist. Of course, His tender heart was torn; but
there was no opportunity for leisure or solitude, because the multitudes needed Him. Out of the wound
in His heart He fed and healed the needy, and thereby
that wound was healed (Mark 6:29-44). Going on
with God always helps and heals.

The "afterward" helps. For every disappointment
there is a delight, for every trial, a triumph; for every
anguish, an "afterward." The Scriptures say explicit-
ly: "Now no chastening for the present seemeth to
be joyous, but grievous: nevertheless *afterward* it
yieldeth the peaceable fruit of righteousness unto them
which are exercised thereby" (Heb. 12:11). God's
hard word is never His last word. The difficulty is
not defeat. The failure of another is not necessarily
a finality. The disappointment need not be disillusionment. The service of Titus did not cease because he
did not arrive at Troas. Rather, it seems that Paul
had even greater need of him in Macedonia than he
had in Troas. The pathway of Christian service, which
we tread with thankfulness to God, assurance of heart,
and encouragement of spirit, may lead to even greater
trials; but the latter bring with them greater triumphs.
Paul was restless in Troas; in Macedonia he found
that "our flesh had no rest, but we were troubled on
every side; without were fightings, within were fears.
Nevertheless God, that comforteth those that are cast

down, comforted us by the coming of Titus" (II Cor. 7:5,6).

Afterward Titus came! It had seemed imperative to Paul that he come to Troas; but for some reason unknown to us, he did not arrive. He was a source of disappointment to Paul, that the latter might learn that life can be a constant pageant of triumph in Christ. With that lesson achieved he learned another, as did Solomon long before him: "Hope deferred maketh the heart sick; but when the desire cometh, it is a tree of life" (Prov. 13:12).

There is the discipline of disappointment that would destroy us, unless we cause it to lift us into a new sphere of usefulness and devotion. Turn from the pain, and find the gain of thankfulness and assurance that will make of your life "a constant pageant of triumph in Christ." Out of heartache there will be healing for you and for others.

> Love grows stronger when assailed;
> Love conquers where all else has failed.
> Love ever blesses those who curse;
> Love gives the better for the worse.
> Love unbinds others by its bonds;
> Love pours forgiveness from its wounds.

God's Handwriting

He writes in characters too grand
For our short sight to understand;
We catch but broken strokes, and try
To fathom all the mystery
Of withered hopes, of death, of life,
The endless war, the useless strife—
But there, with larger, clearer sight,
We shall see this—His way was right.

—John Oxenham.*

*From BEES IN AMBER by John Oxenham. Used by permission of the publishers, American Tract Society, New York.

THE DISCIPLINE OF
DISCERNMENT

"Understanding what the will of the Lord is"
(*Eph.* 5:17).

To see life deeply, as with opened eyes," is the poet's profound and piercing prayer. None of us is free from life's emergencies and exigencies; but we should face them with spiritual insight and uplift. In order to view them with steady eye and untroubled heart we must know whether their source is in the mind of the Almighty or in the machination of Abaddon, the destroying spirit of darkness. Do our circumstances constitute the cross we are to bear daily (Luke 9:23), or a curse from the enemy of man's soul (Luke 13:16); a buffet from an allowed thorn in the flesh (II Cor. 12:7), or a thrust from a fiery dart of the wicked one (Eph. 6:16); a means for searching out our hearts (Rom. 8:27), or a sifting of us by Satan (Luke 22:31); a trial of our faith (I Pet. 1:7), or a temporary triumph of the father of lies (Matt. 13:19; John 8:44)?

Do our troubled feelings mean the conviction of God's gracious Spirit because of our sin (Ps. 32:4), or the condemnation of the implacable accuser of

God's people (Rev. 12:10; I Tim. 3:6)? Is the closed door in our pathway caused by the Holy Spirit (Acts 16:6, 7), or is it a hindrance of Satan (I Thess. 2:18; Rom. 15:22)? Is the apparently open door the plan of the Lord (I Cor. 16:9; Rev. 3:8), or of a lying spirit (I Kings 22:6, 22)? Is our help indeed from angels, sent as ministering spirits (Heb. 1:14), or from the false angel of light, who would lead us into darkness (II Cor. 11:14)? Are we to go onward, strong in the Lord (Eph. 6:10), or to beware of the snare of the fowler (Ps. 91:3; II Tim. 2:26)? Are we to resign ourselves to what appears to be God's will, or to resist what is in reality the design of the devil (both thoughts are contained in the same verse, James 4:7)?

In some way we must be disciplined "to discern both good and evil" (Heb. 5:14), and such discernment should be a work of spiritual maturity (Heb. 5:11-14; Eph. 4:14-16; 6:10-18; Phil. 3:15-19). We are to compare spiritual things with spiritual, in order that our discernment be spiritual (I Cor. 2:12-16). There is a specific gift for "discerning of spirits" (I Cor. 12:10), and altogether too little attention is paid to that heavenly help, to our consternation and confusion. There is then the discipline of discernment, to differentiate between the Spirit of Truth and that of error, the will of God and the working of Satan, the horizon of faith and the hallucination of fanaticism, the promise of the Triune God and the presumption of the tempter.

Truth and error, light and darkness, conviction and condemnation, cross and curse are set in contradistinction, the one to the other, in the Word of God; and there are criteria that constitute this discipline of discernment. Try those touchstones in the fiery trials that now test your faith and courage (I Pet. 1:6, 7; 4:12, 13).

Beelzebub berates us for the blunders we have made; the gentle Holy Spirit speaks of the precious Blood that washes whiter than snow (Isa. 1:18; I John 1:9). The accuser reminded Martin Luther of his many transgressions, and tabulated them. "Is that all?" asked Luther. "No, there are more!" sneered Satan, who added more. "Is that all?" "Yes, and now what?" "No," said the rugged Reformer, "write beneath them all, 'The blood of Jesus Christ cleanseth from all sin.'" The condemnation of Satan points constantly to the sin; the conviction of the Spirit, while not overlooking the stains of the sin, points constantly to the Saviour from sin. Transgression depresses, confession releases (Ps. 32:1-5).

Satan points at self, physical need, social position, self-preservation (Matt. 4:3, 8; 16:23); the Spirit points to the pathway of self-denial and selfless service (16:24-26). The pressure of Apollyon is upon what we want, what we deserve, what is our right, what we can do; the patience of the Unseen Presence points to what we can do for others and what we can do without. Self-pity makes us sulky; self-denial makes us strong in the Saviour. Self-preservation makes us sensitive to imagined slights; complete surrender to the will of God makes us sweet under all circumstances.

The enemy emphasizes the past, with its mistakes and heartaches; the Comforter exalts the present help of our Lord (Ps. 46:1). The devil delights in taunting us with our weaknesses, and the Lord reminds us of the wealth of His riches in grace. Condemnation concerns itself with our failures; conviction shows us the faithfulness of God. The tempter teases us with immediate gain, at any cost; the Trustworthy One tells us of eternal gain, and reminds us of Passion and Patience in Bunyan's House of the Interpreter. The father of lies magnifies our problems, by showing their hopelessness, impossibility, and pain; the God of all grace reminds us of the promises, whereby we can hope against hope; for "tribulation worketh patience; and patience, experience; and experience, hope; and hope maketh not ashamed" (Rom. 5:3-5). Thus we know that pain can mean gain.

The false angel of light would have us walk by sight and earthly wisdom ("the counsel of the ungodly," Ps. 1:1); the Lord of life, who sees the end from the beginning, would have us walk by faith (II Cor. 5:7), and thereby please our Heavenly Father (Heb. 11:6). The enemy would have us see the hosts of evil against us rather than the hillsides covered with ministering spirits (II Kings 6:15-17). He would keep us dwelling upon the injuries from others, until we become ineffective in service, rather than forgetting the things that are behind and pressing forward (Phil. 3:13,14) in the spirit of Him who said, "Father, forgive them." The Vanquished would have us feel the nails and the thorns; the Victor would have us see the triumph of Calvary's tree.

The discipline of discernment requires that we follow the tenets of divine revelation, lest we fall before the wrath of the tempter. We are to meet his subtlety, selfishness and sophistry in the same way as did the Captain of our salvation, with the unequivocal statement, "It is written" (Matt. 4:4, 7, 10). We also are to live by the Word of God, are not to tempt the Lord our God, and are to worship Him only. We are to believe that as we commit our way unto the Lord and trust also in Him, He brings to pass His will (Ps. 37:5). We are to trust that He is able to fill us with the knowledge of His will (Col. 1:9), and to protect us from ways of the destroyer. "When the enemy shall come in like a flood, the Spirit of the Lord shall lift up a standard against him" (Isa. 59:19). As we submit ourselves without reservation unto God, and resist the devil, the latter will flee from us (Jas. 4:7).

By the Word, by the Spirit, by faith, by submission to the divine will, and by resistance to any appeal to self and sin we discern between the way of God and the path of the destroyer.

Friend Unseen

O Holy Saviour, Friend unseen,
Since on Thine arm Thou bidd'st me lean,
Help me, throughout life's changing scene,
By faith to cling to Thee.

What though the world deceitful prove,
And earthly friends and hopes remove;
With patient, uncomplaining love,
Still would I cling to Thee.

Tho' oft I seem to tread alone
Life's dreary waste, with thorns o'ergrown,
Thy voice of love, in gentlest tone,
Still whispers, "Cling to Me!"

Tho' faith and hope may long be tried,
I ask not, need not, aught beside;
How safe, how calm, how satisfied,
The soul that clings to Thee!

—Charlotte Elliott.

THE DISCIPLINE OF
DISCONTENTMENT

"And when the people complained, it displeased the Lord" (*Num.* 11:1).

Bunyan PAINTS a colorful portrait of contentment in his description of the shepherd boy in the Valley of Humiliation, "Now as they were going along and talking they espied a boy feeding his father's sheep. The boy was in very mean clothes, but of a very fresh and well-favoured countenance; and as he sat by himself he sang: 'Hark', said Mr. Great-heart, 'to what the shepherd's boy saith.' So they hearkened, and he said:

"He that is down need fear no fall;
    He that is low, no pride;
He that is humble, ever shall
    Have God to be his guide.

"I am content with what I have,
    Little be it or much;
And, Lord, contentment still I crave,
    Because Thou savest such.

"Fulness to such a burden is,
    That go on pilgrimage;
Here little, and hereafter bliss
    Is best from age to age!"

"Then said their guide, 'Do you hear him? I will dare to say that this boy lives a merrier life, and wears more of that herb called heart's-ease in his bosom, than he that is clad in silk and velvet.'"

"Godliness with contentment is great gain" (I Tim. 6:6) is the divine commentary on this wholesome and healthful attitude of the soul. On the contrary, the danger of discontentment is written large in the Scriptures. Is it fair to infer that godliness without contentment can be great loss?

Discontentment disregards the divine Presence promised to the Lord's own. In their wilderness journey the children of Israel had the pillar of cloud by day and the pillar of fire by night, to go before them in the way (Exod. 13:21, 22), to defend them from their foes (14:19, 20), to show them where they should pitch their tents and when they should journey (Num. 9:15-23): the outward, visible assurance of the Covenant presence. By day or by night they had only to look to the pillar above the Tabernacle, to assure them of God's presence, of His going before them, of His help against their foes. To Moses had been given the strong promise "My presence shall go with thee, and I will give thee rest" (Exod. 33:14). Throughout the long wilderness journey it could be said of Moses, "He endured, as seeing him who is invisible" (Heb. 11:27). Despite the Divine Presence, the people complained (Num. 11:1). "They forgot God their saviour, which had done great things in Egypt" (Ps. 106:21).

In New Testament times we have visible indications of His presence with His people, but we have strong and sure statements by the Saviour: "All power is given unto me in heaven and in earth . . . and, lo, I am with you alway, even unto the end of the world (age)" (Matt. 28:18, 20). That covenant Presence would be by His Spirit, as He explained to His disciples in the upper room: "If ye love me, keep my commandments. And I will pray the Father, and he shall give you another Comforter, that he may abide with you forever; Even the Spirit of truth; whom the world cannot receive, because it seeth him not, neither knoweth him: but ye know him; for he dwelleth with you, and shall be in you" (John 14:15-17). Sweet, wonderful, gracious Presence of the Lord! With us by His Spirit, whom we disregard when we are discontent!

Discontentment despises the promises of God. The children of Israel had been led out of the iron furnace of Egypt by the strong hand of God, to go to the land promised unto their fathers, Abraham, Isaac and Jacob (Exod. 13:3-5). When dissatisfaction gripped their spirit they "despised the pleasant land" (Ps. 106:24), and remembered only "the cucumbers, and the melons, and the leeks, and the onions, and the garlick" (Num. 11:5). Complaint caused them to prefer onions and garlick in Egypt's hard bondage to freedom in a land flowing with milk and honey!

When we are discontent do we not despise our Lord's promises; not only that of His present presence with us, but also of His future provision for us? Did He not say, "Let not your heart be troubled . . . in my Father's house are many mansions"? (John 14:1, 2). When Peter, spokesman for the others, reminded Him, "Lo, we have left all, and followed thee," He replied at once, "Verily I say unto you, There is no man that hath left house, or parents, or brethren, or wife, or children, for the kingdom of God's sake, Who shall not receive manifold more in this present time, and in the world to come life everlasting" (Luke 18:28-30). Ample promises for time and for eternity.

Discontentment discounts the provision God makes for us. For the children of Israel there was daily bread, day by day, in the form of manna, enough for everybody (Exod. 16:4, 14-18). To the hungry and grateful people to whom it came "it was like coriander seed, white; and the taste of it was like wafers made with honey" (vs. 31). When they became disgruntled they could declare with disdain, "But now our soul is dried away: there is nothing at all, beside this manna, before our eyes" (Num. 11:6). By that time "the taste of it was as the taste of fresh oil" (vs. 8). The taste of honey when they were delighted, the taste of fresh oil when they were discontented!

Does that alteration of taste caused by change of attitude seem altogether far-fetched to us; or do we remember seasons when the Word of God is exceedingly sweet to our taste, and when, under the cloud of complaint we find it to be tasteless and commonplace? Honey, or oil, dependent upon our delight in the Word, or our discounting it! Without the Word, how weak and wretched we can feel; with it, how sturdy and strong. "Godliness, *with contentment,* is great gain."

The children of Israel not only discounted the provision of God but also desired the destructive. The divine commentary on their experience says, "They waited not for his counsel: but lusted exceedingly in the wilderness, and tempted God in the desert. And he gave them their request; but sent leanness into their soul" (Ps. 106:13-15). Discontent abounding, desire accomplished, only to turn to destruction of their own good. God deliver us from the "leanness of soul" that proceeds from the persistence of our discontent and insistence on our desire!

Discontentment displeases God (Num. 11:1). Imagine an Israelite, delivered from the bitter bondage of Egypt, led by the pillar of cloud and fire, fed by daily manna, doing anything to displease God his Saviour! It is recorded that the Lord "hath pleasure in the prosperity of his servant" (Ps. 35:27), that He delights to do good always unto them: "For he satisfieth the longing soul, and filleth the hungry soul with goodness" (107:9). It is possible to be a disappointment unto our Lord by not believing Him, for "without faith it is impossible to please him: for he that cometh to God must believe that he is, and that he is a rewarder of them that diligently seek him" (Heb. 11:6). Of Israel it is said, "They believed not his word: but murmured in their tents, and hearkened not unto the voice of the Lord" (Ps. 106: 24, 25). Unbelief that displeased Him; murmuring that hardened their ears to His Voice!

Of the people of Nazareth it is recorded that the Lord Jesus "marvelled because of their unbelief" (Mk. 6:6). They had seen Him in His youth, they had heard of His wisdom and mighty works (6:1); but they had only scorn for Him, saying "Is not this the carpenter?" (vs. 3). Of their attitude the Lord had to say, "A prophet is not without honor, but in his own country, and among his own kin, and in his own house" (vs. 4). Unbelief that made impossible any deeds of mercy in their behalf! Could that not be said of Israel complaining in the wilderness; but what about us who also have the Lord's presence, promises and provision?

Discontentment may be a natural part of our disposition, but contentment can become a major characteristic of our Christian life. The Apostle Paul could testify, "Not that I speak in respect of want: for I have learned, in whatsoever state I am, therewith to be content. I know both how to be abased, and I know how to abound: everywhere and in all things I am instructed both to be full and to be hungry, both to abound and to suffer need. I can do all things through Christ which strengtheneth me" (Phil. 4:11-13). I have learned, I have been instructed, I can do all in Christ—that is the process of achieving contentment. At the very sunset of life the Apostle could say, "Having food and raiment let us be therewith content" (I Tim. 6:8).

The discipline of discontentment is to turn from a complaining spirit, and the criticism that corrodes, from the dissatisfaction that displeases God, to a thankful attitude and "a merry heart (that) doeth good like a medicine" (Prov. 17:22), to the faith and the praise that bring pleasure to the heart of the Almighty. It is to be "content with such things as ye have: for he hath said, I will never leave thee, nor forsake thee. So that we may boldly say, The Lord is my helper, and I will not fear what man shall do unto me" (Heb. 13:5, 6).

Peace, perfect peace, in this dark world of sin?
The blood of Jesus whispers peace within.

Peace, perfect peace, with sorrows surging round?
On Jesus' bosom naught but calm is found.

Peace, perfect peace, with loved ones far away?
In Jesus' keeping we are safe, and they.

—*Edward H. Bickersteth.*

Hush

"Bowed and bended,
Undefended,
Stripped and stunned;
Apprehended
For God's best,
For nature's worst,
For God's rest,
And slacked thirst,
For the deep peace
Undisturbed,
And the heart-throb
Unperturbed —

"Gripped by God
The soul at last
Finds the battle
Is all past.

.   .   .   .   .   .

"Sweet and silent
God-protected;
Closely welded
God-connected
In God's Will —
All is still."

THE DISCIPLINE OF
DISDAIN

"Is not this the carpenter?" (*Mark* 6:3).

THESE QUIET and inconspicuous words do not convey the caustic and causeless criticism contained therein. It was in no complimentary sense that our Lord's fellow countrymen spoke of their neighbor in Nazareth as "the carpenter"; rather it was in consummate and contemptuous disdain that they thus depicted Him. They knew Him as a carpenter; "From whence hath this man these things? and what wisdom is this which is given unto him, that even such mighty works are wrought by his hands?" (6:2) was their query. A carpenter, indeed!

The discipline of disdain tries our mettle as do few searchings of the soul. We may be able to defy intrigue, to disregard innuendo, to deny insinuation; but we find it difficult to endure invective. We dislike to be despised. We cringe at contumely; we become quarrelsome when under contempt.

David and his greater Son, the Lord Jesus Christ, illustrate admirably the discipline of disdain. David met the test many times; and his reactions were not identical in each case. The differences may be accounted for by the occasion or the personalities involved, or possibly by the age at which he endured the discipline. Like him, we all face the cutting contempt that quickens the pulse and kindles the spirit, and by the same token creates the opportunity to show a quiet and Christlike calm.

David defied the disdain of the giant (I Sam. 17: 41-46). He had come from the solitude of the sheepfold, from the struggle with the lion and bear. He was an inconspicuous nobody, unknown and unheralded, with no reputation to maintain nor reward to gain. "And when the Philistine looked about, and saw David, he disdained him: for he was but a youth, and ruddy, and of a fair countenance" (vs. 42). A good-looking, red-headed farmer boy to fight a man of war! A shepherd boy with a staff and slingshot! Jesse's baby with a bag of five stones from the brook! A beardless, barefoot boy to battle with the biggest man in the land! Obviously Goliath could grunt, "Am I a dog, that thou comest to me with staves?" (vs. 43).

The reply to ridicule was a statement of reliance upon God, with no regard for self interest nor reaction to insult: "Thou comest to me with a sword, and with a spear, and with a shield, but I come to thee in the name of the Lord of hosts, the God of the armies of Israel, whom thou hast defied" (vs. 45). No fear for the ferocity of the Philistine, no care for his cursing, no concern for his contempt. David knew intuitively the saying we learned as children, "Sticks and stones may break my bones, but words can never hurt me." Disregard for despising, disinclination to defend self, dependence upon divine aid, this is the discipline of disdain. The heart that can take it walks off with the head of the giant; the spirit that is sweet takes the sword of the swaggering; the trusting bring triumph to many others. Out of disdain comes distinction to him that endures its discipline.

David nearly succumbed to the cynical disdain of Nabal (I Sam. 25:2-13). The aristocrat could say with arrogance, "Who is David? and who is the son of Jesse? there be many servants nowadays that break away every man from his master" (vs. 10). Who is David, the benefactor, the protector, the anointed of the Lord, but a runaway slave, a renegade, a fugitive from justice as far as Nabal was concerned? That is justice for you, gratitude for David's thoughtfulness, appreciation for his solicitude. Just a runaway nobody!

For once David lost his temper. Nabal had been protected by his men, and had now come to sheepshearing time (corresponding in our day to the clipping of coupons, with fleeced folks then as now); and he had berated his own benefactor. To David there was just one solution for such base gratitude: "Gird ye on every man his sword" (vs. 13). David, who had been unmoved by the unjustified jealousy of Saul or the contemptuous cursing of Goliath, could not suffer the sneer of a crusty old sheepherder. Who is David? He carries a burnished sword and a burning heart.

But God, who is rich in mercy, met the embittered David in the person of Abigail (vs. 23-31). She had hastened to restrain his hand from impetuous vengeance. She strengthened his spirit that was sulking before sneering. She depicted the discipline of disdain: regard not this man (vs. 25), forgive any trespass (vs. 28), you are the Lord's own and are doing His service (vs. 28), you have proved yourself patient under other provocation (vs. 28, 29), there will come a day when God's plan is fulfilled in your life; and oh! that in that day "This shall be no grief unto thee, nor offense of heart" (vs. 31).

Would that we might remember in the fire of the injury and the fury of the insult that it is foolish to answer the fool according to his own folly. Therein we become "like unto him" (Prov. 26:4). The fool passes away, his foolishness fades, his sneers cease. By disregarding his disdain and doing our own duty we are masters of ourselves and mindful of tomorrow. David's son could say, "He that is slow to anger is better than the mighty; and he that ruleth his spirit than he that taketh a city" (Prov. 16:32). Yielding to disdain can destroy us; disdaining to yield can delight us.

David met the disdain of Michal (II Sam. 6:20-23). It had been for him a day of gladness: the songs, the sacrifices, the shouting, the sound of the trumpet, the portions to all his people, and above all, the ark of God! "Then David returned to bless his household" (vs. 20). With what radiance and rejoicing he returned. He wanted them to share the blessings of the day. Perhaps he was overly exuberant, unduly excited. Perhaps he needed some restraint in his rejoicing. A smile of approval would have pleased him, a word of kindness would have cautioned him, a note of gratitude to God would have gladdened his heart; instead, there was the measured and miserable meanness of Michal's mimicry, "How glorious was the king of Israel today!" (vs. 20).

It was the same old disdain all over again; Goliath's "Am I a dog?" or Nabal's "Who is David?" But this time it went deeper into the heart of David. Nothing harms like the hurt by one's household, the barb of one's brother, the sarcasm of one's sister, the withering blast by one's wife. From her of all persons David needed sympathy, shelter, assurance, love expressed in "a meek and quiet spirit, which is in the sight of God of great price" (I Pet. 3:4). Instead, he was greeted with studied cynicism and stinging sarcasm. What did it avail to David that for that very day he had composed, by the inspiration of God's Spirit, a portion of Psalm 105 (I Chron. 16:7), in which he had sung God's mighty deeds, His holy name, His covenant with Abraham, His guidance for Israel, the beauty of holiness? What could it mean to David to sing "O give thanks unto the Lord; for he is good;

for his mercy endureth forever" (I Chron. 16:34) when all the while Michal at home "despised him in her heart" (15:29).

The studied scorn of despising, the stinging thorn of disdaining, what a discipline! To sink before its scorching heat is to be in despair; to go onward, even with blistered and bleeding heart is to be disciplined in graciousness and gentleness. One has to imagine the tone of voice in which David made reply to his tormentor, saying, "It was before the Lord" (II Sam. 6:21). Maybe there was anger in the word; rather, I think, it manifested a wounded spirit that committed all to God.

David's greater Son, the Lord Jesus Christ, knew above all others the deep discipline of disdain. Was there ever a heart as tender as His, or a hand as helpful? He went everywhere doing good unto all, and in that ministry of mercy He came to His native village of Nazareth (Mark 6:1-6). There also He offered to be helpful with words of wisdom and healing touch. His efforts were ineffectual, for his hearers would none of Him; rather, "they were offended at him (vs. 3). They summed up their scorn in their caustic query, "Is not this the carpenter?" (vs. 3). To them He was a carpenter, not the Christ; the son of Joseph, not Jesus the Lord. And who can measure the depth of wound caused by the contempt of countrymen and kinsfolk, the known and loved whom He would fain help?

It is the same age-old attitude:
"Am I a dog?"
"Who is David?"
"Is not this the carpenter?"
Disdain that damages or destroys—unless we determine
to dominate our spirit, and to follow in the footsteps
of the Saviour. He could reply with gentleness of
spirit, "A prophet is not without honor, but in his
own country, and among his own kin, and in his
own house" (vs. 4). No censure nor sarcasm in return—only civility and sweetness. He did what good
He was allowed by their antagonism, but no mighty
deed (vs. 5). Their unbelief filled Him with astonishment; but He went onward (vs. 6). There were others
to help, the hungry, the helpless, the heartsick in
other villages.

That is enduring the discipline of disdain: no harsh
reply, no self-justification, no rendering evil for evil.
Rather it is gentleness, goodness, graciousness under
provocation; that we prove ourselves true apprentices
of the Master Carpenter.

In The Hospital

I lay me down to sleep with little thought or care
Whether my waking find me here — or there!

A bowing, burdened head, only too glad to rest,
Unquestioning upon a loving breast.

My good right hand forgets her cunning now;
To march the weary march I know not how.

I am not eager, bold, nor strong — all that is past!
I am willing *not to do*, at last, at last!

My half-day's work is done, and this all my part;
I give a patient God, my patient heart;

And grasp His banner still, though all the blue be dim;
The stripes, no less than stars lead after Him.

—Mary Woolsey Howland.

THE DISCIPLINE OF
DISEASE

"This sickness is not unto death" (*John* 11:4).

FRAIL CREATURES of dust, we are subject to all the fears and frailties of the flesh; not least among which is disease. Abundant, brimming health we accept without a thought of its goodness or any thankfulness to its Giver. Only when illness lays its restraining hand upon our energy and exuberance, when delight gives way to dismay, when song becomes sighing, when days are lonely and nights are long, when strength ebbs and tears flow, do we come to the discipline of disease.

Perhaps the depths of this discipline are not plumbed in the persistence of pain nor the weariness of weakness; rather, in the question that constantly perplexes us: Why this illness? Am I at fault, and therefore to blame for my pain? Is suffering the outcome of my sin; and have I lost all favor with God?

Our sickness may be the result of our own sin. One remembers the words of the Lord Jesus to the man who had been healed, after lying for thirty-eight years at the Pool of Bethesda: "Behold, thou are made whole: sin no more, lest a worse thing come unto thee" (John 5:14). There is no indication of the nature of his infirmity; but the inference seems clear from our Lord's statement that it was brought upon him by himself. And he is not alone in that category. Miriam murmured against Moses, and "became leprous, white as snow" (Num. 12:10). Gehazi coveted the reward from Naaman, contrary to the stated policy of his master Elisha; and he went out "a leper as white as snow" (II Kings 5:27). King Asa had been greatly helped by God in his youth (II Chron. 14; 15); but in later life he trusted his riches and refused the rebuke of God's prophet, with the result that "Asa in the thirty and ninth year of his reign was diseased in his feet, until his disease was exceeding great: yet in his disease he sought not to the Lord, but to the physicians" (16:12). King Jehoram "wrought that which was evil in the eyes of the Lord" (21:6); wherefore Elijah wrote to him, "Behold, with a great plague will the Lord smite thy people, and thy children . . . and thou shalt have great sickness . . ." (21:14,15). Was there some relationship between sickness and sin indicated in the reaction of our Lord to the palsied man, when He said, "Son, thy sins be forgiven thee"? (Mark 2:5).

Not necessarily, however, is infirmity the result of our iniquity. Too quickly we jump to the conclusion that, since some are sick because of their sin, there is, therefore, one cause for illness. How much injustice has been done, how much grief caused, how much sorrow created, because of wrong judgment on the part of the friends or critics of the sick. By inference or assertion they convey the concept that disease arises always from disobedience to the known will of God. The disciples were just like ourselves when they inquired about the man born blind, "Master, who did sin, this man, or his parents, that he was born blind?" (John 9:2).

This unjust and unchristian judgment as to the cause of disease is especially cruel in the case of parents and children. The little ones are impaired in body or mind; and friends and neighbors of the family glance knowingly at each other, or shake their heads in the quiet of their own sheltered homes, to infer, "Must be some reason for that child's condition. A skeleton in the family closet somewhere!"

Such covert criticism is not only unkind, it is cruel, I repeat. The words of the Lord Jesus should have silenced it long ago, but apparently not so. We still go on believing that all sickness can be traced to some specific sin; while He said specifically, "Neither hath this man sinned, nor his parents that he should be born blind."

We cannot afford to be less charitable than our Lord in our compassion for those whose little ones are ill. We cannot fathom the unsearchable wisdom and mercy of God which have allowed this affliction; and we should be prayerful and have pity for the be-

wildered parents, that their hearts be strengthened
and sweetened by the assurance: not because of sin
is this sorrow.

How deep, however, is this discipline of disease
that faces the uncharitable and unchristian criticism
of others because one of ours is ill; and by the same
token, how blessed it is to believe the words of the
Lord Jesus that some illness can be "that the works
of God should be made manifest in him" (9:3). Our
Lord had compassion on the blind man, not caustic
question about his parents; and healed him. What
healing of heart there will be when we learn to be
Christlike in our attitudes!

Sickness can be caused by sin and carelessness on
our part, but not necessarily so; it may be not only
"that the works of God should be made manifest,"
but may even be "for the glory of God" (John 11:4).
That is a strong word: "for the glory of God," and
yet that is what our Lord said of Lazarus and his
illness. We have no indication of the cause of Lazarus'
condition; and we need not infer it was because of
iniquity. Our Lord loved Lazarus (vs. 5), as He does
all His own. In His dealings with us, the Lord chastens
those whom He loves, even scourges His sons and
daughters (Heb. 12:6). The lash of scourging is
not God's last word, however; for although "no
chastening for the present seemeth to be joyous, but
grievous: nevertheless afterward it yieldeth the peaceable fruit of righteousness unto them which are ex-

ercised thereby" (vs. 11). The Psalmist could say, "Before I was afflicted I went astray: but now have I kept thy word" (Ps. 119:67). Again he could sing after prolonged testing, "We went through fire and through water: but thou broughtest us out into a wealthy place" (66:12).

The illness we suffer may not be because of ourselves, but can be from the Enemy. To be sure, we look into the unknown and inexplicable when we seek to trace the source of sickness; but sometimes there seems to be no other possible explanation than: "an enemy hath done this." Again we trace the fears and terror that befell Job, "a perfect and an upright man, one that feareth God" (Job 1:8); and yet to him came devastating, devouring disease. It was allowed of God, in His unsearchable providence; for the Merciful and Mighty One answered the taunt of the Tempter by saying, "Behold, he is in thine hand; but save his life" (2:6). The result was immediate: "So went Satan forth from the presence of the Lord, and smote Job with sore boils from the sole of his foot unto his crown" (vs. 7). So intense was Job's great grief that his friends sat speechless before him for seven days (vs. 13).

Not all sickness is of Satan, just as it is not all because of sin; but the Scriptures say repeatedly that illness can come from the Evil One. The unhappy outcast of Gadara was mentally ill because of indwelling evil spirits; and when the latter were cast out, he sat at the feet of the Lord Jesus, "clothed, and in his right mind" (Luke 8:35). Of a needy one in Galilee the Lord said, "And ought not this woman, being a daughter of Abraham, whom Satan hath bound, lo, these eighteen years, be loosed from this bond on the sabbath day?" (13:16). Of our Lord's ministry it is said that He went about "healing all that were oppressed of the devil" (Acts 10:38). Whatever may have been Paul's "thorn in the flesh," it was "a messenger of Satan to buffet" him (II Cor. 12:7).

It is a part of the discipline of disease to discern its cause, not in impatience or petulance, nor in unbelief; but to seek wisdom from God in the matter. If our sickness is the result of our own sin, we are to repent thereof from the heart, and to commit our ways and days unto God. Our times are in His hands (Ps. 31:15). If Satan is the source, he is to be resisted and refused, that there be deliverance in the mighty name of Jesus. Whatever may be the cause, we are to believe that the pain and weakness can be "for the glory of God," by "life or by death" (Phil. 1:20).

Disease is indeed a hard disciplinarian; and only those under its dominion can know the depths of its discipline. The frailty and futility of it all, the weariness and painfulness, the tears and testings, the long days and longer nights, can cast us into deep gloom, or they can cause us to know the word of the Lord, "My grace is sufficient for thee: for my strength is made perfect in weakness" (II Cor. 12:9). We can, like Paul, also learn to glory in our infirmities, that the power of Christ may rest upon us.

Let us not fear this discipline, nor be defeated by it. Let it search our souls, to see if there be any unconfessed sin therein. Let it show us if our hindrance is from the enemy of souls, that we may be delivered from sin. Let it establish us in the glorious truths that from it we can glorify God and find His grace to be sufficient. Disciplined by disease we can be dispensers of mercy and blessing to many others.

What a friend we have in Jesus,
All our sins and griefs to bear!
What a privilege to carry
Everything to God in prayer.
O what peace we often forfeit,
O what needless pain we bear,
All because we do not carry
Everything to God in prayer!

Reflections

I thank God for the bitter things;
  They've been a "friend to grace";
They've driven me from the paths of ease
  To storm the secret place.

I thank Him for the friends who failed ·
  To fill my heart's deep need;
They've driven me to the Saviour's feet,
  Upon His love to feed.

I'm grateful too, through all life's way
  No one could satisfy,
And so I've found in God alone
  My rich, my full supply!

                              — Florence White Willett.

THE DISCIPLINE OF

DISILLUSIONMENT

"But we trusted that it had been he" (*Luke* 24:21)

How DEEPLY does disillusionment dash to pieces our equilibrium of spirit and our expectation of heart! We all have suffered its sting. Our high hopes, like gallant galleons have sailed afar, and returned not at all, or at best, battered and broken. Our dreams, like high-blown cumulus clouds reaching to the very heavens, have vanished into thin air. We had been confident beyond the slightest contradiction that the consummation of our heart's cry would be contentment; but contrariwise, there came crisis, chaos, and confusion of face. Like the disciples, we had built our life's expectations in the sunshine of Galilee, where crowds had applauded and multitudes had been fed; but there came Gethsemane's shadows, Golgotha's sorrow, and the Garden's silent tomb. Disillusionment, deep, dismal, disintegrating!

What assurance had we that the results of our obedience and sacrifice would be happy? For that matter, what assurance had the disciples? They had left fishing net and counting table, father and mother, household and goods to follow One Who had called with ineffable tenderness, Who spoke as none other, with authority and yet with gentleness, Who fed the hungry and stilled the sea, Who announced a kingdom and its principles, Who provided for every need. Obviously they were sure that He was the Messiah, the Anointed of God, and had built all their life around Him. But now He was dead, dead, and buried, three days ago! Their Messiah, dead; of course they were disillusioned.

Is not that the case with us as far as others are concerned, and to all appearances also at times with the Saviour as well? He became our Saviour from the penalty and power of sin when we received Him as our own, and the Lord of our life. Our Galilee with Him was marked by miracles of grace and guidance, goodness and glory. Samaria saw its service to others, Cana its comradeship, Bethany its blessings, the Temple its teachings; but there came also the shade of olive trees in Gethsemane, the Tree of Calvary, and the Tomb. It seemed that He had failed us, forsaken us forever. Our hearts said mutely, "We trusted it had been he."

The same situation is true as relating to others. Their love had filled our hearts with laughter, their devotion had been our delight, their thoughtfulness had thrilled us, their presence was protection to us, and their person peace. Then came the forgetting, the failure, the forsaking; all to our fear and fainting of heart. Because they were human they were subject to frailty, even with the best of intentions; and because we are human, we suffered because of their failure. Without them life had neither meaning nor motivation, love nor laughter. We were disillusioned.

To face fully the fearful fact of utter loss is the first phase of the discipline of disillusionment. Nothing remains. The Emmaus road, with its disheartened and disillusioned disciples seems ever to have been the portion of God's children all down the ages; yet happy are they who learn its deep discipline.

Abraham learned it on the slopes and summit of Moriah. Isaac, the son of promise, had come at long last into his home and had filled his heart with laughter. Babyhood and childhood had sped by; and Isaac had come to the strength and promise of youth when suddenly there came the heavy shadow of sorrow and loss. The lad was to die; and for Abraham there lay beyond Moriah's summit only the valley of weeping and of withered hopes.

Ruth learned it in the land of Moab. Life had been lovely for her: the homeland, then a stranger from Bethlehem, the courtship, the dreams, the wedding, the new home, the bright vista of a long road together, the love that delights and deepens with the years. But death had rudely dissolved her dreams into dismay; and she stood alone, with aching heart, despairing, disillusioned.

The disciples learned it at the Mount called Calvary. They had believed Jesus of Nazareth to be "a prophet mighty in deed and word before God and all the people," but the chief priests and rulers had delivered Him to be condemned to death and had crucified Him (Luke 24:19,20). Therefore, they added with inexpressible sorrow, "But we trusted that it had been he which should have redeemed Israel: and beside all this, today is the third day since these things were done" (vs. 21). "Trusted," not "trusting," for all hope was gone.

How could they see beyond the Crucifixion to give credence to women's stories about angels and an empty tomb; how could Abraham see beyond Moriah, or Ruth beyond Moab; or we beyond our vale of emptiness and weeping? Disillusionment, deep and final, has become our common lot.

To find that God's hard word is not His last word, that "weeping may endure for a night, but joy cometh in the morning" (Ps. 30:5), is the second phase of the discipline of disillusionment. No careless pruner He, Who spoils the vine; no diffident refiner of silver. For loss He would give us fruit, for dross, silver; far beyond our fondest fancy.

For Abraham on Moriah there was not only the restoration of Isaac, but also the promise, "By myself have I sworn, saith the Lord, for because thou hast done this thing, and hast not withheld thy son, thine only son: That in blessing I will bless thee . . ." (Gen. 22:16).

For Ruth there was not only Boaz, little Obed, and a home in Bethlehem, but also beyond them, David and the Bethlehem Babe, the Saviour Himself after

His humanity. The lonely, sorrowing daughter of Moab became an ancestress of the Messiah!

For the disciples there was not only the exposition of the Word on the way to Emmaus so that their hearts burned within them (Luke 24:27,32), there was also the opening of their eyes to see in reality it was the Lord Himself that walked with them, broke bread in their home. Not only an open Bible, with fulfilled promises, but also a Risen Saviour, the Lord of Life, ever to be present with them, more real and wonderful than He had been even in Galilee!

And for us, in our despair and disillusionment, what provision does He make? Restoration of lost hopes and loved ones like Isaac, with larger promises and deeper acquaintance with Jehovah-jireh, the Lord Who provides; perhaps new blessings, undreamed in our night of sorrow, like Boaz and Obed and the Babe of Bethlehem; perhaps the burning of heart because of His word and the breaking of bread with us day by day in life's pilgrimage.

Disillusionment, designed by the Most High for our good, leads to delight, indescribable and enduring. It is a searching discipline of the soul. It leads to sorrow, suffering, silence and solitude, to the apparently utter loss of the Cross; but beyond that Cross it leads to everlasting gain and good, in time and in eternity. Therefore, let us follow Him fearlessly, obediently, trustingly, until disillusionment is dissolved by delight.

Your Place

Is your place a small place?
Tend it with care!—
He set you there.

Is your place a large place?
Guard it with care!—
He set you there.

Whate'er your place, it is
Not yours alone, but His
Who set you there.

—John Oxenham.*

*From BEES IN AMBER by John Oxenham. Used by permission of the publishers, American Tract Society, New York.

THE DISCIPLINE OF
DISTINCTION

"But when he was strong" (*II Chron.* 26:16).

THERE ARE disciplines of the soul that are deeper and more difficult to learn and that determine character more than do those that are obvious. To be sure, there is the discipline of dismay when we know not which way to turn, but there is also that of delight when the pathway is picturesque and appealing; there is the discipline of darkness when we stand humanly alone in the shadows, and also that of light when we think we walk by sight and not by faith; there is the discipline of difficulty when the road is uphill and when heart fails, but also that of ease when we are drugged into a false sense of security, and like Christian in *Pilgrim's Progress* we sleep in Pleasant Arbor, with consequent loss of time and testimony for Christ; there is the discipline of disease, when in weakness and pain we make our tryst under the shadow of His wing, and also that of health when we seem sufficient to ourselves and think we have little need of Him; there is the discipline of obscurity and neglect when we are overlooked by others, but there is also the discipline of distinction when we come to a place of large opportunity and responsibility.

Disciplines must be learned, inasmuch as they are not naturally a part of our mental and moral make-up. The Apostle Paul could say, "for I have *learned,* in whatsoever state I am, therewith to be content. I know both how to be abased, and I know how to abound: everywhere and in all things I am *instructed* both to be full and to be hungry, both to abound and to suffer need" (Phil. 4:11, 12). The pathway of pleasure and the plains of ease are more dangerous to our spiritual welfare than are the Hill Difficulty and the Valley of the Shadow of Death. There is danger in the terror by night and the pestilence that walketh in darkness; there is also danger in the arrow that flieth by day and the destruction that wasteth at noonday; and these latter are the more subtle and serious.

King Uzziah illustrates the discipline of distinction, and his experience should search out our soul. Of him we read, "for he was marvelously helped, till he was strong; but when he was strong, his heart was lifted up to his destruction." He had begun well. As a youth he carried large responsibilities, and performed them carefully and conscientiously. He would have understood what Jeremiah meant when he wrote later, "It is good for a man that he bear the yoke in his youth" (Lam. 3:27).

Youth has dangers as well as delights; while on the one hand, there is diligence, duty, deference to counsel of elders, and demands that challenge the best in us; there is on the other hand, possibility of defeat. Often young people do not understand themselves nor are they entirely appreciated by others; and happy are you, Sir Youth, and you, Miss Maiden, if you discipline your soul to plan with purpose, to prepare with patience, to study with seriousness, to serve with spirit, to love with lilt of laughter, and to keep looking unto your Lord, the meek and lowly in heart. You will be tempted to take short-cuts that will prove to be dead-end streets, to shoddiness of study and work habits that will be a handicap to you, to selfishness and self-interest that will shrivel your soul and sear your conscience with the thought, "Why do others have accomplishment and ease that I have not achieved?" Youth is the time to study, to struggle, to strive, to serve, to be strong in mind and body, "to bear the yoke."

King Uzziah knew the toil and travail of youth: "He warred against the Philistines . . . he built towers in the desert, and digged many wells . . . he had much cattle . . . he loved husbandry . . . his name spread far abroad" (II Chron. 26:6, 10, 15). In all this, "he did that which was right in the sight of the Lord . . . he sought God . . . and as long as he sought the Lord, God made him to prosper . . . and God helped him against the Philistines . . . he strengthened himself exceedingly" (vss. 4, 5, 7, 8). Blessed is that young person that learns in tender years to trust God and to obey Him, to forget self and to serve others, to lose his life for Jesus' sake, and to find that "them that honor me I will honor," saith the Lord (I Sam. 2:30).

The discipline of distinction comes to us when we have achieved a place of prominence, a plane of privilege a plateau of prosperity, and pleasure of plenty. In prominence do we have the humility of heart that marked us when we followed closely after the meek and merciful Man of Sorrows? Then we perceived that "the meek will he guide in judgment: and the meek will he teach his way" (Ps. 25:9). In privilege do we have the concern for the rights and feelings of others that we had when we were ourselves obscure and unimportant? Then we learned "kindness, humbleness of mind, meekness, longsuffering; forbearing one another, and forgiving one another . . . even as Christ forgave" (Col. 3:12, 13). In prosperity do we have the same tenderness, even tearfulness, of heart and trust in the provision of the God of all grace and comfort that we had when we were penniless in purse and poor in spirit? Then we knew that "the eyes of the Lord are upon the righteous, and his ears are open unto their cry . . . The Lord is nigh unto them that are of a broken heart; and saveth such as be of a contrite spirit . . . none of them that trust in him shall be desolate" (Ps. 34:15, 18, 22).

In our pleasure of plenty do we remember that once we were in painfulness and weariness, that it was of the Lord's mercies that we were not consumed, that His grace was sufficient, that "every good gift and every perfect gift . . . cometh down from the Father of lights, with whom is no variableness"? (Jas. 1:17). Then we learned to take pleasure in the poverty that was rich in faith, in a new portion of physical strength, in provision for daily bread (without pleas for butter and strawberry jam), in prayers that were answered. Now that we have plenty, do we praise God for His many blessings, do we thank Him that our cup is sweet, do we pray for the needy of earth and provide for them out of what God has entrusted to us?

The real test of Christian character comes not when we are toiling to the point of sheer exhaustion; rather it appears when we are exalted and extolled. This is the "arrow that flieth by day," the destruction that may lay waste at noonday. King Uzziah was "marvellously helped, *till* he was strong." But when he was strong, what then? "His heart was lifted up to his destruction: for he transgressed against the Lord his God" (II Chron. 26:15, 16). He could stand poverty but not prosperity, work but not wealth toil but not triumph, struggle but not success, duty but not distinction. His heart was lifted up, only to his destruction.

It is ever so: "Pride goeth before destruction, and an haughty spirit before a fall. . . . He that trusteth in his riches shall fall. . . . When pride cometh, then cometh shame. . . . An high look, and a proud heart, and the plowing of the wicked, is sin" (Prov. 16:18; 11:28, 2; 21:4). The discipline of distinction speaks thus: Are we as tender toward sin as when we knew we were lost? As thankful toward the Saviour as when He saved us? As thoughtful toward others as when we shared a cup of cold water, all we had? As thorough in our study and our service as when we began to tell others about His grace? As trusting in His promises as when we were poor? As trustworthy in our stewardship as when we tithed joyfully our meager resources? Has prominence made us proud; privilege, presumptuous; prosperity, poor in faith; plenty, pitiless toward others? When we have become strong, is our heart being lifted up to our destruction?

The best preparation for the discipline of distinction is the utter contrition of heart that will keep one always contemptible to himself, contrite before the Lord, cautious to hear any appreciation from others, concerned ever with the welfare of others and oblivious of his own pleasure. It is to be taught so deeply by adversity that prosperity is a mercy of the Lord rather than a merit that we deserve. It is to be aware always that whatever may be our success, we are yet "unprofitable servants." It is to be so conscious of the meek and lowly Christ that in our heart we sit at His feet, irrespective of where we may stand in human prominence.

May God grant to us the stern discipline that will enable us to regard distinction as a stewardship to be used in His service, bringing with it deepened dependence upon Him, more definite devotion to duty, disinclination to hear the adulation of others, distaste for the praise of men, death to self-interest, and daily delight in doing His bidding. Thus with increasing lowliness of heart, and love to God and our fellow men, we shall serve Him all of our days, in prosperity or in poverty, in pleasure or in pain, in prominence or in obscurity.

"Father, where shall I work today?"
And my love flowed warm and free.
Then He pointed me out a tiny spot,
And said, "Tend that for me."
I answered quickly, "Oh, no, not that.
Why, no one would ever see,
No matter how well my work was done.
Not that little place for me!"
And the word He spoke, it was not stern,
He answered me tenderly,
"Ah, little one, search that heart of thine;
Art thou working for them or me?
Nazareth was a little place,
And so was Galilee."

Faith

Lord, give me faith!—to live from day to day,
With tranquil heart to do my simple part,
And, with my hand in Thine, just go Thy way.

Lord, give me faith!—to trust, if not to know;
With quiet mind in all things, Thee to find,
And, child-like, go where Thou wouldst have me go.

Lord, give me faith!—to leave it all to Thee,
The future is Thy gift, I would not lift
The veil Thy Love has hung 'twixt it and me.

—John Oxenham.*

*From BEES IN AMBER by John Oxenham. Used by permission of the publishers, American Tract Society, New York.

THE DISCIPLINE OF
DIVERSION

"And as thy servant was busy here and there, he was gone" (I Kings 20:40).

Duty to be performed may be difficult, dreary, even dangerous; but it is delight when it is done. There are many dangers between detail of duty and "Well done, good and faithful servant"; and not least among the dangers to be defined and denied is that of diversion. We remember the old fable of the race between the tortoise and the hare; and while we admit we are not so patient as the plodder who won the encounter, we disagree that we are as stupid as the sleepy-head that lost. The danger of diversion from the plain path of duty is always with us; and at no time should we be over confident of our powers and progress toward the goal.

Diversion from duty may come by sheer carelessness on our part. The prophet who spoke in parable to King Ahab painted a very human picture. A responsibility had been entrusted to him, and he had been irresponsible. "Thy servant went out into the midst of the battle; and, behold, a man turned aside, and brought a man unto me, and said, Keep this man:

if by any means he be missing, then shall thy life be for his life, or else thou shalt pay a talent of silver. And as thy servant was busy here and there, he was gone" (I Kings 20:39,40). He was familiar with military discipline. He understood his task. He knew the consequences of carelessness, but he was careless, nevertheless. Careless in conduct, derelict in duty, he had endangered both himself and his country.

How large is this lesson written in the life of young people, and their elders, also, to be sure. The assignment is clear, the time-limit is exacting, the reward is definite as is the penalty, in case of failure. Diversion, however, lurks in the uphill climb to success, not necessarily wicked things, just carelessness, idleness, day-dreaming, the radio, a bull-session, a magazine article, even a long letter that has its place, but not first place when duty calls. There was every intention to do the work, to finish the assignment, to be faithful to one's trust; but they were undisciplined in denying themselves leisure or luxury, just "busy here and there" with trivialities until the hour-glass of opportunity had emptied itself and the task was unfinished. The better is often the enemy of the best; and we are busy with good things, important activities, helpful enterprises, but not the duty we are to do now. College students are tempted to substitute the extra-curricular for the curricular, the social for the academic, the easy for the difficult, the interesting for the essential, the recreational for the creative, the better for the best. Everything worthwhile has its time and place, but not the same time nor place. Beware lest by being "busy here and there" we get nowhere.

Diversion from duty can come through dangers of the way. Daniel had his duties, secular and divine. In both he was eminently faithful, to the consternation of his foes. Anyone who comes to a place of responsibility in the world or in God's service faces unreasoning and unrestrained envy. Daniel was faithful and effective, and was given the place of highest authority (Dan. 6:1-3). The court politicians "could find no occasion nor fault" (vs. 4), until they remembered his daily worship. By craftiness they got the king to make illegal worship of any kind for a period of thirty days, with a penalty attached for violation, severe enough to cause anyone to think twice before transgressing the decree.

Daniel saw through their subtlety and subterfuge, and knew that his testimony as a man who feared God was at stake. From the outset of his service in the court of Babylon he had maintained consistently that the living God was his helper. To Nebuchadnezzar he had said, "There is a God in heaven that revealeth secrets" (2:28). On a later occasion he warned the king, "till thou know that the most High ruleth in the kingdom of men" (4:25). To the blasphemous Belshazzar he could say sternly, "Let thy gifts be to thyself, and give thy rewards to another. . . . O thou king, the most high God gave Nebuchadnezzar thy father a kingdom, . . . and the God in whose hand thy breath is, and whose are all

213

thy ways, hast thou not glorified" (5:17,18,23). In the new time of trial, with windows of lattice open to the view of all, "he kneeled upon his knees three times a day, and prayed, and gave thanks before his God, as he did aforetime" (6:10).

The remainder of the story is very familiar: the lurking of his enemies to spy upon him, the lion's den, and the hand of God stretched out in approval on the conduct of His servant. The dangers we face may not be so dreadful as were those of Daniel, and the deliverance may not be as dramatic; nevertheless we face the possibility of diversion from our duty by danger to ourselves or our own. Happy is that heart that is faithful in his responsibilities to God and his fellow men and that can say, "The Lord is my helper, and I will not fear what man shall do unto me" (Heb. 13:6). Disciplined to do one's duty despite any danger!

Diversion from duty can come from undue emphasis on the unnecessary details of the duty. One recalls the lovely old story of our Lord in the home of Lazarus, Mary, and Martha (Luke 10:38-42). How welcome He was in their home, to share their large-hearted hospitality. Of Mary it is recorded, "which also sat at Jesus' feet, and heard his word" (vs. 39). Too much can be made of the little word "also," but it may mean, that in addition to her duties, quickly and quietly accomplished, she had time to listen to the Master. For that, Martha was too busy; and at length she felt she had to lodge a complaint with the Lord, saying, "Lord, dost thou not care that my sister hath left me to serve alone? bid her therefore that she help me" (vs. 40).

I am sure that every earnest and faithful worker appreciates Martha's position in this matter. She had a right to expect help. After all, was not the Guest of guests in the home, and should He not have the best?

Our Lord's answer is very illuminating: "Martha, Martha, thou art careful and troubled about many things: *But one thing is needful*" (vss. 41,42). Many efforts have been made to discern deeply what our Lord meant in His word to Martha, but those I have read miss the point of His statement. He knew a woman's heart, and her desire to do her very best for her Guest; but He preferred more fellowship and less food, more conversation on things everlasting and fewer courses, more listening and less luxury. *"But one thing is needful:* just something simple, a one-course dinner: soup, or stew, (or if it were in our day) just a salad or waffles." Something easy to prepare, so that there will be time and strength to talk of spiritual things, the "good part, which shall not be taken away" (vs. 42). Diverted from duty and delight by details, interesting but necessary. Too occupied with the trees to see the forest, too fussy about food to have fellowship with our guests, too much serving to listen, too many good errands to run a straight course, too much Martha and too little Mary. We can do much, and yet miss "that good part."

Diversion from duty can also come from preoccupation with the past, with its successes and failures. The Apostle Paul had been caused to remember his heritage and training, his earnest efforts to achieve the righteousness of the Law of Moses (Phil. 3:6), all of which seemeth worse than useless "for the excellency of the knowledge of Christ Jesus my Lord" (vs. 8); so that he could say with conviction, "this one thing I do, forgetting those things which are behind, and reaching forth unto those things that are before, I press toward the mark for the prize of the high calling of God in Christ Jesus" (vss. 13, 14).

He had natural reason to view with pride and pleasure the position and place that were his by heritage. He could have dwelt in detail on the advantage of the Jew in knowledge of the Old Testament, in the promises, in the orthodoxy of the Pharisee. Contemplation of his family connections could have led to ancestor worship, which practice in modern times is not restricted to some Chinese. Some are so preoccupied with the past: its benefits, blessings, bounties, that they forget there is a future goal to which they should be striving at the present time. Looking backwards they run an uncertain and hazardous course.

The opposite can also be the case: we can be so grieved by the mistakes and galled by the failures of the past that we have no heart for the present or the future. We prefer to sit alone by life's roadside, to hug the heartache to ourselves, to review our recklessness, to weep over opportunities, to berate our embittered heart. The long shadow of the past allows no sunshine on our path, repeated failures predict new ones in the future, old flaws can never be mended, the past has swallowed up the present and the future: so we reason with morbid memory, not remembering we are to forget the past. It is gone, it is under the Blood, it is committed unto Him Who has said in His Word, "Who is a God like unto thee, that pardoneth iniquity, and passeth by the transgression of the remnant of his heritage? he retaineth not his anger forever, because he delighteth in mercy. He will turn again, he will have compassion upon us; he will subdue our iniquities; and thou wilt cast all their sins into the depths of the sea" (Mic. 7:18, 19). The past, with its pride and its shame, alike cast into the sea of God's forgetfulness, so that we, "forgetting those things which are behind, and reaching forth unto those things that are before . . . press toward the mark for the prize of the high calling of God in Christ Jesus"!

Disciplined not to be diverted from the pathway of duty by present carelessness or impending dangers, by multitude of daily details or the long shadows of the past; this is the discipline of diversion we need that we too can say, "This one thing I do!"

217

Make me a captive, Lord,
   And then I shall be free.
Force me to render up my sword,
   And I shall conqueror be.
I sink in life's alarm
   When in myself I stand;
Imprison with Thy mighty arm,
   Then strong shall be my hand.

My heart is weak and poor,
   Until its Master finds;
It has no spring of action sure,
   It varies with the winds.
It cannot freely move
   Till Thou hast wrought its chain;
Enslave it with Thy mighty love,
   Then deathless I shall reign.

—George Matheson.

THE DISCIPLINE OF
DOMINATION

"Thy gentleness hath made me great" (Ps. 18:35).

Most of us are followers, and rightly so, but it is the responsibility of some to assume leadership for the welfare of the many in the school or the church, the farm or the factory, the community or the nation. Of the followers it is required to be diligent and cheerful in the performance of our duties; for the leaders there is the discipline of domination that analyzes the attitudes and measures the motives of those who are called to places of authority, lest they lead or rule for self-interest. Do we lead with love for others and with loyalty to the lowly Christ, or do we lord it over them? With true and searching insight into the human spirit, the Lord Jesus Christ said to His disciples, and through them to us, "Ye know . . . they that are great exercise authority upon them. But it shall not be so among you: but whosoever will be great among you, let him be your minister; And whosoever will be chief among you, let him be your servant: Even as the Son of man came not to be ministered unto, but to minister, and to give his life a ransom for many" (Matt. 20:25-28).

There are few stories of rising from obscurity to authority more signal than that of David, who was taken from the humble calling of caring for sheep to becoming king of his country. Modern fiction and biography have interesting annals for us to consider, but none quite equals the achievement of the youngest son of Jesse. A peasant lad became a prince, a singer saved his people with a slingshot, a poet performed deeds of valor, a country boy became a king, a shepherd boy became a sovereign. What was the secret of such startling success, that we might learn therefrom?

Our first response would undoubtedly refer to his courage as the cause for his achievement. Who when gazing in some zoo at a bear or a lion has not remembered that David met such creatures bare-handed, and has realized that supreme courage is needed in such encounter? Devotion to duty, as exemplified in guarding his father's sheep from the depredations of wild animals; or magnetic leadership, which is the endowment of some men, might be other touchstones of his triumph; but to none of these does David make allusions in recounting with all humility his rise to authority. He said simply and candidly, "Thy gentleness hath made me great."

Who would have guessed that gentleness, meekness, docility, mildness of spirit gave true meaning to David's life? He appears to be a carefree, courageous keeper of sheep, a fearless soldier and magnificent leader of men, a man of war rather than a maker of peace; in brief, a man whose military prowess made him master of his people; nevertheless, these qualities were not the true secret of his greatness. Meekness made him a monarch, kindness made him a king, gentleness made him a great man in the earth.

He was gentle toward his own. For example, when consumed with thirst in the confines of Adullam's cave, he sighed aloud, "Oh that one would give me drink of the water of the well of Bethlehem, that is at the gate!" (I Chron. 11:17). Three of his devoted soldiers, at risk of life and limb, broke through the lines of the Philistines to draw water from that well and to bring it to their captain. In profound appreciation for their love and loyalty, he would not drink thereof, but rather poured out the water as an offering unto the Lord. To him it represented their very lifeblood, because they had ventured their lives in order to please him. Who would think that within the breast of a stern soldier like David would lie such gentleness of spirit toward his own?

One recalls an incident somewhat analogous thereto in the course of the first World War. The lads of the outfit told me of an incident that had occurred before I joined them. The First Division had been relieved after arduous agonizing service on the Argonne front, and had been relieved to go to a rest area; only to be turned back into the lines within the space of a few hours. There had developed imminent danger of a break-through by the enemy. As the weary and battle-worn doughboys returned through a destroyed French village, the Stars and Stripes were flung into the breeze, the Regimental Band was drawn up amid the debris of the market place; and the Brigade Commander reviewed his troops as they returned to the trenches. To martial music and to colors of Red, White and Blue they marched "eyes-right" passed their General, to see tears coursing down his cheeks, tears of tenderness for his tired men. General Frank Parker was a tough West-Pointer, but within he had tenderness of a woman's heart.

Do we have that gentleness of spirit toward our own, those of our own household, those closest to us, whom easily we can injure by thoughtless word or act; those alongside in the work of our Lord, who share our responsibilities and are of like frailties with ourselves. We cannot be caustic to mother and truly courteous to others, critical of father and really considerate of lover, unkind in home or church and genuinely consistent in testimony for Christ. Tenderness is a true test of leadership, a discipline of domination.

David was likewise *gentle to his enemies,* those who despitefully used and abused him. There are few characters so unworthy and ungracious as Saul, first king of Israel. Out of sheer jealousy he sought to destroy the young man who had delivered his people from the yoke of the Philistines, and who had brought peace and prosperity to his nation. He hunted David like a wild partridge in the wilderness, so that there was but a step between him and death. At length, there came opportunity for David to reply in kind to his king; but he would not. Saul slept, as did his servants; and David drew near in the silence and shadows to find his relentless foe. More than once Saul was at David's mercy, whose companions urged him to avenge himself, or at least to allow them to do so for him, but David would not. "The Lord forbid that I should do this thing unto my master, the Lord's anointed" . . . "Who can stretch forth his hand against the Lord's anointed, and be guiltless?" (I Sam. 24:6; 26:9). In effect David performed the precepts given long afterward by the Lord Jesus, "Love your enemies, bless them that curse you, do good to them that hate you, and pray for them which despitefully use you, and persecute you; That ye may be the children of your Father which is in heaven" (Matt. 5:44, 45).

Are we possessors of a gentleness so genuine that we can be patient toward our persecutors, gracious to the ungrateful, charitable to the churlish, tender-spirited toward our tormentors? Are we disciplined in domination, rulers of our own spirit before we are rulers of others? "He that is slow to anger is better than the mighty; and he that ruleth his spirit than he that taketh a city" (Prov. 16:32). "Dearly beloved, avenge not yourselves, but rather give place unto wrath: for it is written, Vengeance is mine;

223

I will repay, saith the Lord. Therefore if thine enemy hunger, feed him; if he thirst, give him drink: for in so doing thou shalt heap coals of fire on his head" (Rom. 12:19, 20).

Above all, David was *gentle toward God*. He had a sensitivity of spirit to the presence, the power, and the providence of the Most High. He recognized that it was not his hand nor his strength that saved him from the bear and the lion, rather it was of the Lord; even from Goliath; for "the battle is the Lord's" (I Sam. 17:47). From experience he could say, "My soul, wait thou only upon God; for my expectation is from him. He only is my rock and my salvation: he is my defence; I shall not be moved. In God is my salvation and my glory: the rock of my strength, and my refuge, is in God. Trust in him at all times; ye people, pour out your heart before him: God is a refuge for us" (Ps. 62:5-8).

Especially do we see this gentleness of spirit in the story of David and Nabal. The latter was a wealthy sheepherder, whose possessions David and his men had protected. In return they asked a small favor of Nabal, but Nabal railed upon them. Then David seemed to show something of the spark that in his disposition could be stirred on occasion, and for the moment he forgot the gentleness that maketh great. David's reaction was, "Gird ye on every man his sword" (I Sam. 25:13). In anger he determined that no Nabal would deny him his due reward. Ingratitude and injustice were intolerable to the tender-hearted David. This was too much!

In the meantime the incident had come to the attention of Abigail, Nabal's wife, who hastened to make amends by bringing food for David and his men. She pleaded with him not to avenge himself, rather to commit his cause to the Lord that judgeth righteously. She reminded him that his days were "bound in the bundle of life with the Lord thy God; . . . That this shall be no grief unto thee, nor offense of heart unto my lord, either that thou hast shed blood causeless, or that my lord hath avenged himself" (vs. 29, 31). To be sure, he had no need to pay attention to her plea, but he recognized therein the rebuke of the Most High. With true humility and gentility he responded, "Blessed be the Lord God of Israel, which sent thee this day to meet me; And blessed be thy advice, and blessed be thou, which hast kept me this day from coming to shed blood, and from avenging myself with my own hands" (vss. 32, 33).

Herein is perhaps the greatest test of true gentleness: a sensitivity of spirit that recognizes that we are liable to error of attitude or act, and that God in His faithfulness will seek to restrain us through some servant of His. We are reminded of our sonship, for our life is "hid with Christ in God" (Col. 3:3), of our social relationship, for hereby "shall all men know that ye are my disciples, if ye have love one to another" (John 13:35). We are caused to remember that "the triumph of the wicked is short" (Job 20:5), and that God has an "afterward" for His chastened children (Heb. 12:11). How wonderful it is to have no regrets because of temper when we come to triumph and reward!

Do we have the gentleness to heed the counsel of another, to take graciously the word or rebuke about our own course of action or the suggestion that our spirit may not be right, that we have not been guided of God in this detail? David could say, "Let the righteous smite me; it shall be a kindness: and let him reprove me; it shall be an excellent oil, which shall not break my head" (Ps. 141:5).

Gentleness of spirit toward those who are close to us, gentleness toward those that wrongfully abuse us or are our enemies, gentleness toward the Spirit of God, through whatever means He may speak to us, this is the discipline of domination. Uprightness of character and tenderness of heart are imperative prerequisites for those upon whom devolves the leadership of others. Among his last words David included that truth, saying, "He that ruleth over men must be just, ruling in the fear of God. And he shall be as the light of the morning, when the sun riseth, even a morning without clouds; as the tender grass springing out of the earth by clear shining after rain" (II Sam. 23:3,4).

We remember again David's statement that whatever success had come to him was because "Thy gentleness hath made me great." It was not his native tenderness, personality, nor ability; rather it was God, whose Spirit in his life was manifested by gentleness, "The fruit of the Spirit is love, joy, peace, longsuffering, gentleness" (Gal. 5:22).

It is the gentleness of the indwelling Saviour, the tender, compassionate Jesus, shown forth to others by His Spirit of grace. Gentle to our own, to our enemies, and especially to God, this gentleness that maketh great.

The lovely things are quiet things—
Soft falling snow,
And feathers dropped from flying wings
Make no sound as they go.
A petal loosened from a rose,
Quietly seeks the ground,
And love, if lovely, when it goes,
Goes without sound.

The Pruned Branch

"Every branch that beareth fruit, he purgeth it, that it may bring forth more fruit."

It is the branch that bears the fruit
    That feels the knife,
To prune it for a larger growth
    And fuller life,

Though every budding twig be lopped
    And every grace
Of swaying tendril, springing leaf
    Be lost a space.

Oh, thou whose life of joy seems reft,
    Of beauty shorn,
Whose aspirations lie in dust,
    All bruised and torn,

Rejoice, though each desire, each dream,
    Each hope of thine
Shall fall and fade; it is the hand
    Of love divine

That holds the knife, that cuts and breaks
    With tenderest touch,
That thou, whose life hast borne some fruit,
    May now bear much.

               —Annie Johnson Flint.*

*From POEMS by Annie Johnson Flint. Used by permission of the publishers, Evangelical Publishers, Toronto.

THE DISCIPLINE OF

DOUBT

"Blessed is he, whosoever shall not be offended in me" (Matt. 11:6).

Doubt, like dismal, dank darkness, settles down upon our spirit; and benumbed with bewilderment, we know not what to do nor what road to take. Doubt, like deep-seated disease, gnaws ceaselessly, remorselessly at the vitals of our convictions and conscience; and dizzy with dismay, we falter and faint. We doubt ourselves and our friends, our background and our future, our experience and the facts thereof, our faith in the Bible and the God it presents. Doubt defeats, discourages, destroys.

By way of sharp contrast, faith builds, lifts, lightens, strengthens. "The just shall live by faith" (Heb. 10: 38; Rom. 1:17). Faith brings lilt of laughter for sighing of sorrow, light of life for darkness of despair, strength of spirit for faltering of fear, balm of blessing for hunger of heart. They who believe are blessed: happy, joyous, steady, strong, whose resources are from unfailing springs of refreshing.

Many Beatitudes are familiar to us, as Psalm 1:1, 2, "Blessed is the man that walketh not in the counsel of the ungodly, nor standeth in the way of sinners, nor sitteth in the seat of the scornful. But his delight is in the law of the Lord; and in his law doth he meditate day and night." From childhood we have known, "Blessed are the poor in spirit . . . they that mourn . . . the meek . . . they which do hunger and thirst after righteousness . . . the merciful . . . the pure in heart . . . the peacemakers . . . the persecuted" (Matt. 5:3-12). Do we know also the blessing of believing, so that we do not stumble?

By way of illustration, we trace the experience of John the Baptist and of Thomas the Doubter. Who can fathom the depths of despair depicted in John's question, "Art thou he that should come, or do we look for another?" (Matt. 11:3). Had he not received clear and convincing revelation that Jesus was the Lord, the Son of the Highest? He knew from the Word that he himself was "the voice of one crying in the wilderness, Make straight the way of the Lord" (John 1:23). He could say boldly, "I baptize with water: but there standeth one among you, whom ye know not; He it is, who coming after me is preferred before me, whose shoe's latchet I am not worthy to unloose" (vss. 26, 27). He saw the Spirit descend upon Him as a dove, and heard the voice from height of heaven, "This is my beloved Son, in whom I am well pleased."

How could revelation by the Word and by the Spirit be more real and certain? John knew beyond shadow of doubt that Jesus was the Christ, the Lamb of God that taketh away the sin of the world; and still he came into dungeon of Doubting Castle. We have equally valid testimony by Word and by Spirit, that "all Scripture is given by inspiration of God" (II Tim. 3:16) . . . that although "All have sinned" we are "justified freely by his grace" (Rom. 3:23, 24) . . . that "As many as received him, to them gave he power to become the sons of God" (John 1:12), that "hereby we know that he abideth in us, by the Spirit which he hath given us" (I John 3:24); yet to us also, as to the Baptist, comes the deep discipline of doubt.

Whence this shadow over spirit, this searching of soul, this chastening of character, this manacle of mind, this hopelessness of heart? The Forerunner's experience is informative and enlightening. We, like him, can come under the heel of an implacable Herod, physical or spiritual, until we begin to wonder, "Lord, art thou he?" The *loss of health* is a stern and cruel jailer of the soul. Blinding pain and lingering weakness make dim the delights of yesterday, and like David we complain, "In the day of my trouble I sought the Lord: my sore ran in the night, and ceased not: my soul refused to be comforted . . . thou holdest mine eyes waking: I am so troubled that I cannot speak . . . will the Lord cast off forever? . . . doth his promise fail forevermore? . . . hath God forgotten to be gracious?" (Ps. 77:2-9).

The *loss of happiness* can dig deep into the human spirit. Like John we have known the sweetness of human fellowship, the strength of human love, the satisfaction of service rendered unto the Saviour and our fellow men, yet for beauty of bountiful blessings we have ashes of anguish and absence, for strength through oil of His joy we have weakness through multiplied mourning, for praise caused by His providence and protection we have heaviness and hopelessness and helplessness. Our soul has entered into iron; lover and friend are far from us; and we seek to fathom the fearful shadows by crying, "Art thou he, or look we for another?"

The loss of hope can cause one to come under the crab-tree cudgel of Giant Despair, whose incessant blows leave us bruised, bloody, beaten. We stagger to rise and to shake off our doubts and fears, but to what end, and by what means? There is no hope, we say to ourselves; rather, we concur with the poet:

"Truth forever on the scaffold,
    Wrong forever on the throne."

We cannot vindicate ourselves nor get others to help us. We realize no alleviation of circumstances, much less justice. If it were anyone but that "Herod" in my life; but there he is, mocking, merciless, mighty. We are brought into the net. Men ride on our heads. We go through fire and water; and we begin to wonder, "Lord, art Thou He? Dost Thou care?"

The loss of holiness can also bring us into the darkness of despair and doubt. There is no indication in John's experience that it was because of disobedience or sin that he found himself in Herod's dungeon.

Often, however, in human experience we find that unbelief does have a moral cause. We know the will of God, yet we desire our own way. We sense the conviction of the Spirit because of our wrong, but we love our sin. We are dark of mind because we are hard of heart. We doubt because we disobey. We run through red lights of warning—moral, physical, spiritual; and find ourselves doubting the mercy of the Most High because of our own wilfulness and waywardness. We stumble because we sin, even though we know, "He that covereth his sins shall not prosper; but whoso confesseth and forsaketh them shall have mercy" (Prov. 28:13).

Doubt may derive from disease or from derangement of bodily function, from disposition to moodiness because happiness is gone, from despair that good can ever come out of evil, from disobedience that enthrones self and eclipses the Saviour. Whereas, formerly we had rejoiced in the sweetness of His salvation and the sunshine of His presence, now we doubt His Word, character, faithfulness, power, perhaps even His Person, and say in substance, "Art thou he, or look we for another?"

The first step back from doubt to faith is to bring one's plight to the Lord Jesus Himself. It is no sin to ask a question if our heart attitude is right. The Lord Jesus himself asked "Why hast thou forsaken me?" not in unbelief, but in perfect trust and submission. Resolutely we must turn from self and any known sin, from weakness or weariness, to Him in all candor and good conscience. He does not despise nor willingly afflict His own. His heart is touched with compassion because of our need. He wants us to come to Him, to obtain mercy in time of need. Take your doubt and difficulty to Him, as did John.

The next step is to believe the evidence He presents. To John He sent word of His deeds and words; to Thomas He stated, "Reach hither thy finger, and behold my hands . . . be not faithless, but believing" (John 20:27). Believe what He has done for you, and for others down the ages. His Word has stood the test of the centuries, and will stand the caustic criticism others may now be casting at it. God's mercy is new each morning, and is everlasting; His grace is sufficient, His faithfulness will not fail. He tries His children but does not tempt them to despair; He burns the dross from their life as does a refiner of silver, but He does not abandon them. Believe His power to strengthen you, His presence to help you, His peace to keep you, His providence to care for you.

The third step from darkness of doubt to delight of faith is to believe His Word. "Faith cometh by hearing, and hearing by the word of God" (Rom. 10:17). The Lord Jesus answered the thrusts of doubt from the Tempter, "If thou be the Son of God . . ." with ringing "Thus saith the Lord, It is written . . . it is written" (See Matt. 4:3-11). To take one's stand on the Word of God, to believe what He has promised, all appearance to the contrary notwithstanding, to be steadfast, unmovable, unafraid, to ignore the insinuations that cast clever and calculated criticisms against the character of the God of all grace, is to find oneself strong in the Lord. Believe your beliefs that are founded upon the Word, and doubt your doubts that come from disease, despair, disappointment, or disobedience. Doubt paralyzes; faith vitalizes. Doubt defeats; faith triumphs. Doubt destroys; faith makes alive. To the evidences that will come to your tested and trusting soul there will be the response of Thomas, "My Lord and my God"; and you will be partaker of the blessing to the unoffended, who "have not seen, and yet believed" (John 20:28, 29).

Honest doubt, faced by the Word of God and faith, will discipline your heart and mind to bring you into deeper devotion and assurance.

Wilt Love Me? Trust Me? Praise Me?

O thou beloved child of My desire,
Whether I lead thee through green valleys,
    By still waters,
      Or through fire,
Or lay thee down in silence under snow,
Through any weather, and whatever
        Cloud may gather,
        Wind may blow —
Wilt love Me? trust Me? praise Me?

No gallant bird, O dearest Lord, am I,
That anywhere, in any weather,
        Rising singeth;
        Low I lie.
And yet I cannot fear, for I shall soar,
Thy love shall wing me, blessed Saviour;
        So I answer,
        I adore,
I love Thee, trust Thee, praise Thee.

—Amy Carmichael.*

*From TOWARD JERUSALEM by Amy Carmichael. Used by permission of the publishers, Society for Promotion of Christian Knowledge, London.

THE DISCIPLINE OF
DURABILITY

"For he endured, as seeing him who is invisible"
(*Heb.* 11:27)

Tensile strength is the real test of endurance. To be torn unmercifully by external forces, and still to preserve one's poise and position, and especially one's inward integrity, is to know the discipline that endures. It is one thing to run when the opposition rises, to hide when the danger terrifies, to reply when the word is unkind or untrue; it is quite another thing to stand still in order to see the Lord's salvation or to hold one's tongue by committal of everything to Him who judges righteously.

Moses learned this discipline in the disillusionment of the desert. Egypt had proved to be a mirage to him. Pharaoh's household had been no spiritual help. "Sonship" with Pharaoh's daughter had been no satisfaction to his innermost soul. Court etiquette had not created endurance of character. He had renounced his position to identify himself with his despised fellow countrymen; but they had spurned him. The dreary distances of the desert supplied the solitude he needed for the suffering of his soul.

One day, however, the discipline of the desert was at an end; and the service for God and man was thrust upon Moses. From out the burning bush there came the command: "I have surely seen the affliction of my people. . . . Come now therefore, and I will send thee unto Pharaoh, that thou mayest bring forth my people the children of Israel out of Egypt" (Exod. 3:7,10). To Pharaoh, from whom he had fled; to Israel, who had despised him? Surely not; that he could never do. He had failed once; inevitably he would do so again. With reason he could protest, "Who am I, that I should go unto Pharaoh, and that I should bring forth the children of Israel out of Egypt?" (vs. 11).

To that plea there was but one reply on the part of the Most High: "Certainly I will be with thee" (vs. 12). Whatever would be the perplexities and problems, indignities and impossibilities in the undertaking at hand, Moses could count upon the presence of God; and because of that Presence he could "endure as seeing him who is invisible."

Moses endured despite the cold, cutting contempt of Pharaoh. The mightiest monarch of that day could say to the meekest of men, who came with the message of God, "Who is the Lord, that I should obey his voice?" (Exod. 5:2). Royalty had no regard for the Redeemer of Israel or for His servant, Moses; the sovereign had no sense of the divine imperative upon the shepherd from Midian. The crown had only contempt for the command of God and for the complaints of God's people, saying, "I know not the Lord, neither will I let Israel go" (5:2).

Contempt can cut deeply into our spirit and cause us to waver from the course of action we believe to be of God, if we allow the contempt to lodge within our breast. Contrariwise, it cannot confuse us if we keep our eyes upon the Lord, and continue steadfast in our persuasion of His precept and promise. We can endure contempt from worldlings, great and small, if we keep our eyes on the Crucified. "If ye be reproached for the name of Christ, happy are ye; for the spirit of glory and of God resteth upon you" (I Pet. 4:14). Count on Christ when others hold you in contempt!

Moses endured, despite the causeless complaint of the multitude (Num. 11). By the strong hand and stretched-out arm of God the children of Israel were brought out of the fiery furnace of Egypt. By that same hand they had been led through the Red Sea, and had received water from the flinty rock, had been provided daily manna for their physical needs, had been given the Law from the fiery summit of Sinai, and had with them the constant reminder of the Divine Presence in the pillar of cloud by day and of fire by night. What needed they more?

Nothing; and yet they complained. They had food, ample, wholesome and palatable; but they complained, "Who shall give us flesh to eat? We remember the fish, which we did eat in Egypt freely; the cucumbers, and the melons, and the leeks, and the onions, and the garlick . . ." (Num. 11:4, 5). They could remember Egypt's leeks, but not its hard labor, the cucumbers, but not its cruel bondage; its garlick, but not its garrisons of sadistic soldiery; its fish, but not its Pharaoh. Long memory they had for precarious food supply in Egypt, and a very short memory for the provision God had made for them every day of their pilgrimage.

How deeply can unreasoned and unreasonable complaint of the people penetrate the spirit of their leader. Their cry is constant although causeless, their weeping is woeful, their distress is disturbing to others, until all the camp is a bedlam of abuse against the leader. Then to him came the decision: to endure or to despair, to stand firm or to sink beneath the accumulation of complaint, to follow God at all cost, or to fall before the "gripers." Moses was exceedingly moved by the misery created by the complaint, even to the extent of crying unto God in secret, "I am not able to bear all this people alone, because it is too heavy for me" (11:14). In His grace and graciousness God told him to gather seventy elders of Israel, to the end that "they shall bear the burden of the people with thee, that thou bear it not thyself alone" (vs. 17). As to the complaint of the people for flesh, God added, "Is the Lord's hand waxed short?" (vs. 23). Moses could endure the causeless and constant complaint of an unbelieving people, because beyond them he could see that Invisible Being Who had promised, "My presence shall go with thee, and I will give thee rest" (Exod. 33:14). Long centuries before the day of David, the sweet singer of Israel, and before that of Simon Peter, who quoted David's psalm, Moses knew the assurance of such words as these: "The eyes of the Lord are over the righteous, and his ears are open unto their prayers . . . and who is he that will harm you, if ye be followers of that which is good?" (I Pet. 3:12, 13; Ps. 34:15). *Count on Christ when others complain!*

Moses endured, despite the criticism of some who were closest to him (Num. 12). A man can ignore to a large extent the contempt of the worldling and the complaint of the weakling, but he cannot belittle the blows and bruises that come from his own flesh and blood. "Miriam and Aaron spake against Moses" (12:1). This time it was sister and brother against the saint of God, not the insincere and bewildered mob. The latter had complained about food, with lust for leeks and garlick; Miriam and Aaron made criticism of Moses' family. Such criticism can cut a man to the quick, even one like Moses who was "meek, above all the men which were upon the face of the earth" (12:3). No hurt can be so deep as that caused by one's household; no barb so bitter as that of one's brother.

The Lord Jesus knew the suffering entailed in the treachery of trusted ones when He spoke of "a man at variance against his father, and the daughter against her mother. And the daughter-in-law against her mother-in-law; and a man's foes shall be they of his own household" (Matt. 10:35, 36). He knew what it was to have His friends seek to take Him away from the needy multitude, because they believed, "He is beside himself" (Mk. 3:21). Later they came with His mother to take Him, and called Him from afar (Mk. 3:31). Has anyone ever suggested, even remotely, that you are a bit unbalanced mentally, because of your zeal for God's service? Then you have some idea of the inner suffering that can come from the thought that your closest friends think you are growing insane. Our Lord's brothers said to Him in scorn, "Depart hence, and go into Judea, that thy disciples also may see the works that thou doest"; because "neither did his brethren believe in him" (John 7:3, 5). We are not above our Master, and if He suffered the unkind and caustic criticism of His own, as did Moses, so also shall we. Count on the *Compassionate Crucified to help you when cherished ones criticise!*

Moses endured, despite the confusion and condemnation created by the fearful leaders who had spied out the land of Canaan (Num. 13:26-33). The latter had seen the land of promise, which truly flowed with milk and honey (13:27). Every prospect of the land was pleasing, but the people thereof appeared too strong for any contemplated invasion; with the result that the ten spies "brought up an evil report of the land" (13:32). Despite the protestations of Caleb and Joshua, the children of Israel "wept that night . . . and . . . murmured against Moses and against Aaron . . . And they said one to another, Let us make a captain, and let us return into Egypt" (14:1, 2, 4).

It is at that hour of confusion and condemnation on the part of others that the discipline of durability comes strongly to any leader of men. With much insight into human nature did Rudyard Kipling write his undying challenge to every man:

If

If you can keep your head when all about
    Are losing theirs and blaming it on you;
If you can trust yourself when all men doubt you,
    But make allowance for their doubting too;
If you can wait and not be tired by waiting,
    Or, being lied about, don't deal in lies,
Or, being hated, don't give way to hating,
    And yet don't look too good, nor talk too wise;

If you can dream—and not make dreams your master;
    If you can think—and not make thoughts your aim;
If you can meet with triumph and disaster
    And treat those two impostors just the same;
If you can bear to hear the truth you've spoken
    Twisted by knaves to make a trap for fools,
Or watch the things you gave your life to broken,
    And stoop and build 'em up with wornout tools; . . .

If you can talk with crowds and keep your virtue,
  Or walk with kings—nor lose the common touch;
If neither foes nor loving friends can hurt you;
  If all men count with you, but none too much;
If you can fill the unforgiving minute
  With sixty seconds' worth of distance run—
Yours is the Earth and everything that's in it,
  And—what is more—you'll be a Man, my son!

To keep one's head when all are losing theirs, and casting all the blame onto you — that is the hour to endure, in the strength of Him Who "endured such contradiction of sinners against himself" (Heb. 12:3). *Count on the Cross-bearing Christ, the Author and Finisher of our faith, when others condemn you!*

The contempt of the world, the complaint of the crowd, the criticism of loved ones, and the condemnation of the fearful; are not these enough to discipline the soul in endurance? Moses knew more than these; and so shall we. There came the cold, cunning conspiracy of Korah, Dathan, and Abiram, who caused two hundred fifty princes to follow them against Moses (Num. 16:1-3). These princes were not a rabble; they were regarded as "famous in the congregation, men of renown" (16:2). Their complaint is characteristic of the criticism of lesser men all down the ages: their leader assumed too much authority (16:3). They may have seemed to be big men to their contemporaries; actually they were contemptibly small men. Only big men know how to obey implicitly their leader and to perform cheerfully their tasks. Small men demand authority because they do not deserve it.

It is an accurate index of a man's inward endurance to face without fear or fury the conscience-less and contemptible conspiracy of trusted men, and to believe that God will vindicate the right. The crisis may be critical, so that we like Moses are bowed to the ground (16:4); and the judgment upon the unfaithful may be with finality, as it was for the cabal of Korah (16:30-33); but God will not fail His own when conspirators seem to prosper. "Evildoers shall be cut off: but those that wait upon the Lord, they shall inherit the earth. . . . I have seen the wicked in great power, and spreading himself like a green bay tree. Yet he passed away, and, lo, he was not: yea, I sought him, but he could not be found" (Ps. 37:9, 35, 36). *Count upon Christ when they conspire to cast you out of your appointed place.*

This is the discipline of durability: to endure "as seeing him who is invisible" when all manner of cruelty is concocted against you: contempt, complaint, criticism, condemnation, or conspiracy. The Invisible Christ will not fail you. Walk as in His presence; and find His power, provision and protection from all evil. Having done all, stand!

Not in Vain

Not in vain the tedious toil
On an unresponsive soil,
Travail, tears in secret shed
Over hopes that lay as dead.
All in vain, thy faint heart cries,
Not in vain, thy Lord replies;
Nothing is too good to be;
Then believe, believe to see.

Did thy labour turn to dust?
Suffering—did it eat like rust,
Till the blade that once was keen
As a blunted tool is seen?
Dust and rust thy life's reward?
Slay the thought: believe thy Lord,
When thy soul is in distress
Think upon His faithfulness.

—Amy Carmichael.*

*From TOWARD JERUSALEM by Amy Carmichael. Used by permission of the publishers, Society for Promotion of Christian Knowledge, London.

THE DISCIPLINE OF
DUTY

"Doing the will of God from the heart" (*Eph.* 6:6).

Is THERE delight deeper or more delectable than that of duty diligently done? To know one's responsibility, to face its circumstances, both favorable and unfavorable, to follow the line of duty without deviation caused by difficulties or distraction, and to fulfill the task as assigned — all this brings great joy. Between finding out our task and fulfilling the same there lies the discipline of duty, often arduous and difficult, even to the point of impossibility.

By way of illustration, we follow the experience of the Apostle Paul in the fulfillment of his assignment, "for as thou hast testified of me in Jerusalem, so must thou bear witness also at Rome" (Acts 23:11). To the trusting and obedient child of God, there is the gracious possibility of being "filled with the knowledge of his will in all wisdom and spiritual understanding; That ye might walk worthy of the Lord unto all pleasing" (Col. 1:9,10). We are not to be "unwise, but understanding what the will of the Lord is" (Eph. 5:17). There is gracious provision for guidance by the Lord who is our Shepherd (Ps. 23:1), who "when he putteth forth his own sheep, he goeth before them, and the sheep follow him: for they know his voice" (John 10:4). It has always been so with the people of God: Abraham was called to inherit a land he had not seen, Joseph was to become the ruler and benefactor of his brethren, Moses was to lead his enslaved people from the iron furnace of Egypt, David as a shepherd boy was anointed to be king over Israel, Cyrus the Persian was to order the restoration of Jerusalem, Mary was to see a performance of those things told her from the Lord, and Paul was to witness also in Rome. For you and me as for them, the will of God calls us to our duty.

The Wrath of Men. Immediately that there is knowledge of God's will for your life there will be opposition thereto. The enemy of man's soul will do all in his power to thwart the purpose of the Most High. A conspiracy of wicked men plotted on the very next morning to take Paul's life (Acts 23:12,13). When David became king, "all the Philistines came up to seek David" (II Sam 5:17). When Nehemiah sought to rebuild his city, the adversaries were present with intimidation, innuendo, intrigue, and insinuation, to resist his efforts. However, it may not be wicked men who oppose your way, but even good hearts and true may misinterpret God's will for you, and like Peter, say "far be it from you." The Pharisees and Herodians sought to destroy the Lord Jesus (Mk. 3:6), and also His friends "went out to lay hold on him: for they said, He is beside himself" (3:21).

What says the Word of God on such circumstances? "The fear of man bringeth a snare: but whoso putteth his trust in the Lord shall be safe" (Prov. 29:25). Nehemiah could say, "should such a man as I flee?" (Neh. 6:11). "He hath said, I will never leave thee, nor forsake thee. So that we may boldly say, The Lord is my helper, and I will not fear what man shall do unto me" (Heb. 13:5, 6). "No weapon that is formed against me shall prosper; and every tongue that shall rise against thee in judgment thou shalt condemn. This is the heritage of the servants of the Lord, and their righteousness is of me, saith the Lord" (Isa. 54:17; note also Isa. 41:10-13; Ps. 31:17-21; 37:7-11).

The Lord has a way of escape for His tried, yet trusting child. His help is sure, but His methods are seldom guessed. A lad overheard the plot of Paul's persecutors, and the Apostle's life was spared. Goliath was overcome by a shepherd boy with sling and stone, Mordecai's record was read to the restless King after Haman had erected the gallows, four unknown lepers opened "windows in heaven" to feed the hungry of Samaria (II Kings 7), and so it goes. God is not without a way to shield your life from the "strife of tongues" (Ps. 31:20), and to set you free from the wrath of men.

Waste of Years. The determined and crafty adversary of your soul will not desist from his opposition to the will of God in your life after one defeat. Paul was taken from Jerusalem to Caesarea on his way to Rome, only to languish for an undefined and interminable period. There was no case against him, but he had no friends at court, nor would he stoop to bribery (Acts 24:26); with the result that he remained immobile in the dungeon. His soul entered into delay and darkness, caused by the negligence and selfishness of others.

That experience is not uncommon among the children of God. Moses was rejected by his people and spent forty years in the wilderness, David was hunted as a partridge on the hillside of Judea by an insanely jealous Saul, Elijah sat by the brook and later shared the hospitality of a heathen home when Ahab ruled in the land, and Paul in his earlier life spent years of obscurity in Arabia and Tarsus. Are you also entering into this experience described by David? "I was a reproach among all mine enemies, but especially among my neighbors, and a fear to mine acquaintance: they that did see me without fled from me. I am forgotten as a dead man out of mind: I am like a broken vessel" (Ps. 31:11, 12). Never fear; there is no neglect so complete nor indifference so studied that can stultify the will of God for your life, if you will trust Him in the lengthening shadow of years apparently wasted. The silence of the dungeon will make sweeter and stronger the song of deliverance.

Waves of Despair. Paul did not perish in prison, for God made a way to escape from that Doubting

Castle. It was a strange way, perhaps from a human point of view an unnecessary way. He was compelled to appeal to Caesar (Acts 25:10-12), though in reality there was no legal means therefor (26:32). Thus it is that indifference on the part of others comes to an end. Moses is called of God to go down into Egypt, Elijah is sent to Ahab, Paul at Tarsus is called to Antioch. When God's hour strikes, you will go forward into His will, not perhaps as you had planned but in a way which He sees is best for you. Paul had long been desirous of "a prosperous journey by the will of God to come" to Rome (Rom. 1:10). God allowed it to be a perilous journey for His spiritual prosperity and also for ours.

The adversary was not without devices when he had failed by wrath of men or waste of years to thwart God's will for Paul; nor is he without methods to divert you from the center of that will. As a prisoner, Paul was taken aboard ship to be brought to Rome. In reality he was the prisoner of the Lord (Eph. 3:1; 4:1); and that attitude makes all the difference in the world. As His prisoners we need not fear the yoke of men. Our legal rights may be trampled under foot, our sound counsel may be scorned (Acts 27:11), and we find ourselves the apparent victim of circumstances into which comes a storm so overwhelming that "all hope that we should be saved was then taken away" (27:20).

How about that? Years before, God had said to Paul, "Rome"; now the enemy sneered, "drown." Is that true of you today with all human hope gone, and only the consciousness deep in your soul that God did make plain to you His will, and to the best of your knowledge and ability you have obeyed Him?

Paul's experience of the grace of God under such circumstances can also be yours. There came a message to his innermost being, "Fear not, Paul; thou must be brought before Caesar" (Acts 27:24). It was much like the experience of the terrified disciples in a storm on Galilee when they heard, "Be of good cheer: it is I; be not afraid" (Mk. 6:50). The process was the same in both instances: the Lord was taking the storm out of the life of His children before He took them out of the storm. God grant that amid the roar of the wind and the raging of the sea of your life that you may hear anew the still, small voice of His spirit saying, "Be not afraid, thou must fulfill his will." "And so it came to pass, that they escaped all safe to the land" (Acts 27:44).

The Wickedness of the Adversary. Had not God's servant endured enough difficulties in the pathway of duty? The enemy did not think so. He might escape the wrath of men, the waste of years, and the waves of despair, and therefore must be destroyed by direct attack. "There came a viper out of the heat, and fastened on his hand" (Acts 28:3). There was no escape from snake bites, only certain death.

How does the Serpent attack God's children? Perchance by sickness as was the woman whom he had bound eighteen years (Luke 13:16), by self-pity

(Matt. 16:21-25), by self-sufficiency so that we fall into "condemnation of the devil" (I Tim. 3:6), "for Demas hath forsaken me, having loved this present world" (II Tim. 4:10).

Suddenly, swiftly the adversary strikes to render us ineffective in God's service, and thus bring to an inglorious end the will of God for our life.

When he strikes, we must be strong in the Lord, filled with the Spirit, under the precious blood, walking in obedience unto God and in service to men, so that we also can shake him off into the fire and feel no harm (Acts 28:5). With us as with Paul such experience will be a testimony to others of the saving and keeping power of our Lord, and we ourselves shall be stronger because of His salvation. There will come the moments of fulfillment of the will of God, "and when we came to Rome" (28:16). We should share even now the assurance that Moses knew, "My presence shall go with thee, and I will give thee rest" (Exod. 33:14); the strength that Joshua knew, "Be strong and of a good courage; be not afraid, neither be thou dismayed: for the Lord thy God is with thee withersoever thou goeth" (Josh. 1:9); and the sweetness that Paul knew, "And the Lord shall deliver me from every evil work, and will preserve me unto his heavenly kingdom: to whom be glory forever and ever" (II Tim. 4:18).

The Discipline of Duty is not easy nor light, its performance is painful and perilous, but its culmination is delight.